This book is part of a 3 book series which comprises:

- DVSA Revision Theory Test Questions and Guide to passing the Driving Test Combined Edition published in 2018

- DVSA Revision Theory Test Questions and Guide to passing the Driving Test and Truckers Handbook Combined Edition published in 2018

- The Essential New Truckers Handbook published in 2016. Updated 2019

Buyers should note the truckers handbook in part is incorporated in:

- DVSA Revision Theory Test Questions and Guide to passing the Driving Test and Truckers Handbook Combined Edition published in 2018

The Essential New Truckers' Handbook

MALCOLM GREEN

THE CHOIR PRESS

First published in the United Kingdom in 2015 by The Choir Press
Revised 2016 and 2019

ISBN 978-1-78963-046-6

The author fully acknowledges the crown copyright of; www.highwaycodeuk.co.uk'updated 2018', as the sauce for all road signs and symbols used in this publication. Found in Chapter 21.

The author fully acknowledges the crown copyright of; www.gov.uk/guidance/ drivers-hours-goods-vehicles', as the sauce of information used in chapter 3.

The author fully acknowledges the crown copyright of; www.assets, publishing service.gov.uk/.../simplified-guide-to-lorries-types-and-weights-2003, as the source of information used in chapter 14.

The author fully acknowledges the crown copyright of;www.gov.uk/ drivers hours and tachographs, goods vehicles in GB and Europe 'updated 2017 ', as the sauce of information used in chapter 16.

The author fully acknowledges the crown copy right of; www.gov.uk/government/publications/load-securing-vehicle-operator-guidance/load-securing-vehicle-operator-guidance'updated 2017' as the sauce of information used in chapter 27.

Contents

Preface

My aim with this handbook is to help new drivers into work, by explaining the minefield of procedures and technology. This book is also an attempt to simplify the rules and regulations in a bid to keep a driver and his/her hard-won licence safe from harm. I am an LGV1 driver, still currently driving, with 24 years in the industry. I therefore have the requisite experience to write a handbook such as this. I understand the job very well and have made great efforts to impart as much depth of knowledge as possible in order to help you to avoid making mistakes as you go forward with confidence into a new career.

This handbook is an insight into what to expect and what will be expected of you. 'Forewarned is forearmed.' I have made a great effort to create a comprehensive, user-friendly guide. This book should be accessible, whether you are just starting out in the industry, returning after an absence of leave, or simply wish to brush up on the ever-changing rules and regulations. For matters of ease, I have used articulated vehicle images to illustrate various procedures. Everything translates into all categories of LGV vehicles.

Note:

Do not be daunted.

This book is fairly comprehensive. As a beginner the only chapters you really need to focus on and get to grips with are:

1, 2, 3 ,4, 5, 6, 7, 10, 11, 12, 14, 17, 21, 25, 26.

Chapter 1

Tachograph and Digicard

Introduction

This chapter focuses on the tachograph unit that truck drivers must use as an everyday part of their job. It includes a step-by-step guide of how to enter a manual entry, plus various information on the driver's digicard, which must be inserted into the tachograph unit.

One important reason why the manual entry procedure was introduced was in order to give DVSA (the Driver and Vehicle Standards Agency) proof that mandatory checks have been undertaken.

The fifteen minutes at the start of the shift during which the tachograph must be set to 'other work' (the cross hammers symbol) covers you in the event of an inspection. DVSA takes this as proof that vehicle inspection checks have been carried out.

I have provided a detailed easy to follow guide, which I hope will make things easier.

It is a bit complex at first, but, after completing it a few times, it will become second nature. Before you get the hang of it, if you are really struggling, you might want to try this alternative (plan B) strategy:

- Press OK on the tachograph vehicle unit (VU) to all questions asked.

- Once this is completed, change the tachograph symbol to 'other work' (crossed hammers).

- **Now do not move the truck for 15 minutes, whilst you carry out vehicle checks.**

Users Guide to Manual Entry
- Siemens Tachograph Unit

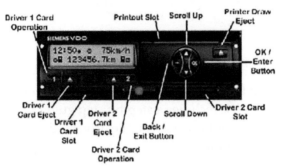

Symbols ʰ = Rest Period. ˣ = Other Work. ◳ = POA ☉ =Driving

  The pictures on either side of this text show an example of a driver's card. The picture on the left shows the driver's details and photo ID. The one on the right shows the chip and the direction that the card needs to be inserted into the tachograph.

Step 1)   Turn on ignition and one of these screens will appear.

A)
17:07	☉	0km/h
X	123456.7km	h

B)
!☉◳ driving	
without card	28

If box "B" 'driving without a card' appears', press OK.

Step 2)   Insert your driver's card in card slot 1, making sure that the chip is facing forward and upward, and then wait for

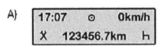

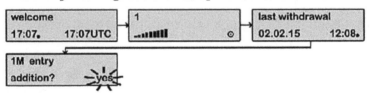

The above sequence will happen automatically. When the last screen appears, the 'yes' symbol will be flashing. Press OK to proceed.

Step 3) The next screen **(A)** shows the date and time that the card was last withdrawn on the top line. It also shows the date and time that the card has been inserted today on the bottom line. The 'rest' symbol will be flashing.

Now follow these steps in order using the up, down forward and back buttons.

Change the symbol to 'other work' X, and press OK.
Change the date to the last shift date and press OK.
Change the time to the last shift finish time and press OK.
After completion of these steps you will arrive at screen **(B)**.

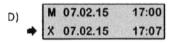

Now **(C)** change the time to the start time of today's shift and press OK. Then **(D)** Change the symbol to 'other work' X and press OK.

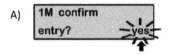 

Step 4) A) Confirm manual entry and press OK.

B) Begin country, press OK.

C) The final screen, you are now ready to go.

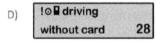

Note: If box "D" 'driving without a card' appears', press OK.
If you make a mistake at any time, press the back button.
Warning, once you confirm manual entry, there is no going back.

Driver's Digicard Information

A driver digicard stores information on dates and times worked, vehicles driven, duty periods, rest etc.

It expires after 5 years. To apply for a new card, you must complete the form D777B/DL that is available from the DVLA.

The card will retain information for 28 working days. This information needs to be downloaded before the 28th day to avoid the information being overwritten.

If the card appears to be malfunctioning it is worth trying it in another vehicle to establish if the card is at fault.

Always remember your digicard, as, unless it is lost or stolen, it is illegal to drive the vehicle without it.

Do a printout at the end of each day.

Lost/stolen digicard:

If the card is lost or stolen you must apply for a new one within 7 days. Following an application for a new card, you are able to drive without it for a maximum of 15 consecutive days (not working days).

If the card is stolen, this must be reported to the police and a crime reference number obtained.

Whilst waiting for your new digicard you must keep manual records. At the start of a shift, press print on the tachograph. On the printout, you must write down the vehicle's licence plate registration number. You must also write down enough information to identify you as the driver of the vehicle. For example, driver's licence number, driver card number and signature. Also, include your shift start time and the actual time you started driving.

At the end of a shift, press print on the tachograph. On the printout, write down the vehicle's licence plate registration number along with all periods of other work (whether you were in the vehicle or away from it), periods of availability and rest. Then ensure again that you include enough information to identify you as the driver.

Remember that these printouts count as official work records. As the driver, it is your responsibility to make sure that all work records are able to be understood easily and kept clean and presentable.

By law, it is required that you keep this printout with you for 28 days before handing it in to the company. If the company asks to retain it at the end of your shift, then you should photocopy it. If you are stopped by DVSA, they will want to see it.

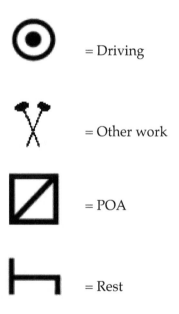

= Driving

= Other work

= POA

= Rest

Note: It is advisable to help to gain an understanding of doing a 'manual entry' by going on you tube and looking at videos posted by lgv drivers to help new drivers.

Useful you tube videos:

Siemens digital tachograpgh – manual entry)
(The rockgod23)
https://www.youtube.com/watch?v=3Al6H0LuQBE&t=12s

Stoneridge digital tachograph –manual entry
(The rockgod23)
https://www.youtube.com/watch?v=Ei4e4yu-YDM&t=230s

Chapter 2

Official Working Time Regulations (WTR)

Introduction

The aim of this chapter is to give you all the important information regarding WTRs. Subjects are subtitled and bullet pointed for ease of reference.

These EU regulations were introduced in April 2005. They are a bit of a double-edged sword. On the one hand, they add restrictions and put pressure on drivers by adding a second set of times and breaks to adhere to. On the other hand, these regulations safeguard drivers against being exploited – forced to work too many hours. They also ensure that drivers are entitled to definite breaks every 6 hours.

To newcomers, the information in this chapter may seem a little daunting at first. Don't let this faze you. I have made sure to explain the essential parts of these overcomplicated regulations in as simple and comprehensive a manner as possible. In Chapter 3, under 'Drivers' Hours Rules simplified', point 7, 10 and 11 will be helpful until you get a good grasp of these complicated rules.

Working Time Regulations (WTR)

Hours of work:

- Drivers are required, on average, to work no more than 48 hours per week.

- This average is calculated over a period of time, known as a 'reference period'.

- One working year (52 weeks) is made up of three reference periods: two reference periods which last 17 weeks and one reference period which lasts 18 weeks.

- In this way, the three reference periods add up to a full working year: $17 + 17 + 18 = 52$.

- Please be aware that these stipulations may be slightly altered if you are part of either a 'collective agreement' or a 'workforce agreement'.

  o A collective agreement is an amendment to standard working time regulations which is reached via negotiation between an employer and a trade union.

  o A workforce agreement is an amendment to standard working time regulations which is reached via negotiation between an employer and workforce representatives.

- There are two possible amendments to standard working time regulations concerning reference periods. Having a 'fixed reference period by agreement' means that:

  o Start and end dates of reference periods can differ from the standard industry dates.

- The average weekly working hours can be calculated over two 26–week reference periods, rather than three reference periods.

- These two reference periods will still add up to a full working year: $26 + 26 = 52$.

- Having a 'rolling reference period' means that:

  - A continuous, weekly updating average is taken over the previous 17 weeks. The first 17-week period of work is calculated in the standard way; however, after this the average is updated weekly. For example, in the 18th week, the average is calculated over the 17-week period spanning working weeks 2–18.

- Despite being required to work no more than 48 hours per week on average, you may work anywhere up to 60 hours in any single week starting at 00.00 on a Monday morning.

- You may not exceed more than 10 hours in any single 24-hour period if you are working at night. The night work limits can only be exceeded where there is a work force or collective agreement in place.

  - If driving a goods vehicle, you are legally considered to have worked a night shift if you have worked between 00.00 and 04.00.

  - If driving a passenger-carrying vehicle, you are legally considered to have worked a night shift if you have worked between 01.00 and 05.00.

- Rest Breaks – a driver must not work for more than six hours without a break. If a driver works six-to-nine hours, they need a break or breaks totalling at least 30 minutes. If a driver works more than nine hours, they must have a break or breaks totalling 45 minutes. Break duration should be of at least 15 minutes. Any breaks can be divided into 15 minute periods.

Weekly rest:

- WTR requires the driver to take 45 consecutive hours' weekly rest. This can be reduced to 24 hours providing that any reduction is made up for within 3 weeks.

Periods of availability (POA):

- POA is waiting time, the periods of which should be known in advance.

- POA criteria:

    o The mobile worker should not be required to remain at work-station (typically the vehicle).

    o The mobile worker must remain available to answer calls and resume work on request.

    o The duration of POA must be known in advance. Either before departure or just prior to the start of period in question.

Useful tips:

- If you do enter into either a collective or workforce agreement:

    o Make sure you find out exactly how this will affect you and alter your weekly duties.

    o Ensure that you keep in contact with other employees to ensure that your understanding of this agreement matches theirs.

- If it is your contractual duty to calculate your own working time:

    o Make sure to subtract rests, breaks and POAs from your total time worked.

- Make sure to subtract any sick days, holidays etc. from your total time worked.

- Remember, keeping accurate daily written records will help you in this task.

- Ensure that all records are kept (filed or backed up on a computer for at least two years).

Information on Multi-Manning

'Multi-manning' is the situation where during each period of driving between any two consecutive daily rest periods, or between a daily rest period and a weekly rest period, there are at least two drivers in the vehicle to do the driving. For the first hour of multi-manning the presence of another driver or drivers is **optional**, but the remainder of the rest period is **compulsory**. This allows for a vehicle to depart from its operating centre and collect a second driver along the way, providing this is done within 1 hour of the first driver starting work.

Vehicles manned by two or more drivers are governed by the same rules that apply to single-manned vehicles, apart from the daily rest requirements.

Where a vehicle is manned by two or more drivers, each driver must have a daily rest period of at least 9 consecutive hours within the 30-hour period that starts at the end of the last daily or weekly rest period.

Organising a drivers duties in such a fashion enables a crew's duties to be spread over 21 hours.

This is an example of how the duties of a two man crew could be organised to take maximum advantage of multi-manning rules.

	Driver 1	Driver 1
3	Daily Rest	Daily Rest
0	Other work 1 hour	Daily rest (not on vehicle) 1 hour
	Driving 4.5 hours	Availability 4.5 hours
H	Break +availability 4.5 hours	Driving 4.5 hours
O	Driving 4.5 hours	Break+ availability 4.5 hours
U	Break+ availability 4.5 hours	Driving 4.5 hours
R	Driving 1 hour	Break+ availability 1 hour
S	Break 1 hour	Driving 1 hour
	Daily rest (9 hours)	Daily rest (9 hours)

The maximum driving time for a two man crew taking advantage of this concession is 20 hours before a daily rest is required (although only if both drivers are entitled to drive 10 hours)

Under multi-manning, the 'second ' driver in a crew may not necessarily be the same driver from the duration of the first driver's shift but could in principle be any number of drivers as long as the conditions are met. Whether these second drivers could claim the multi-manning concession in these circumstances would depend on their other duties.

On a multi-manning operation, 45 minutes of a period of availability will be considered to be a break, so long as the co-driver does not work.

Other than the daily rest concession detailed above drivers engaged in multi-manning are governed by the same rules that apply to single-manned vehicles.

Journeys involving ferry or train transport

Where a driver accompanies a vehicle that is being transported by ferry or train, the daily rest requirements are more flexible.

A regular daily rest period, that is one of 11 hours duration or 12 hours if split, may be interrupted no more than twice, but the total interruption must not exceed 1 hour in total. This allows for a vehicle to be driven on to a ferry and off again at the end of the crossing. Where the rest period is interrupted in this way, the total accumulated rest period must still be at least 11 hours or 12 hours if split. A bunk or couchette must be available during the rest period.

Drivers who are engaged on multi-manning can also interrupt a rest period however they may only do so where the rest period in the 30 hour spread over is a regular daily rest of at least 11 hours or 12 hours if it is a split daily rest.

Any rest that is interrupted must be completed within the 24 hour period (if Any rest that is interrupted must be completed within the 24 hour period (if single manned) or within the 30 hours period (if multi-manned). The 24 or 30 hour period commences at the point of starting duty following the end of a daily or weekly rest period.

It is also permitted to have one of the interruption periods falling in the 3 hour part of the split rest period and one interruption period falling in the 9 hour part of the split rest period or for both parts of the interruption period to fall within the 3 hour part of the split daily rest.

Chapter 3
Drivers' Hours Rules

Introduction

This chapter is split into three parts. The first section is the official drivers' hours rules. Don't worry if you find this a little confusing as, in the second section, I give a simplified, concise version of this information. This will hopefully make the first section a little easier to understand. The second section will also allow you to revise the relevant information whenever you need to. The third section contains some tips and advice regarding drivers' hours rules.

Note: the information contained in this chapter is of the most importance with regards to keeping your license safe and needs to be adhered to at all times.

Drivers' Hours Rules (official version)

Driving period

A driving period is the accumulation of actual driving time between two break periods or following a rest period.

Daily driving time

You may not exceed 9 hours' actual driving time per day. However, this can legally be extended to 10 hours twice a week. Doing this makes no difference to the rest of your weekly actual driving hours.

Weekly driving time

You should not exceed 56 hours in total.

Fortnightly driving time

You should not exceed 90 hours' total driving time in any two consecutive weeks.

Break periods

After 4½ hours of continuous driving have elapsed, an uninterrupted break of 45 minutes must be taken.

A break of 45 minutes can be replaced by a 15-minute break followed by a 30-minute break. You could, for example, drive for 2 hours, take a 15-minute break, drive for a further 2½ hours and then take a 30-minute break. During this break period, you may not legally do any form of work (even written work).

Please note, however, that you may not take a 30-minute break followed by a 15-minute break. This is to ensure that you are properly rested for your next period of driving.

Daily rest

Daily rest can be reduced from 11 hours to 9 hours three times a week. Doing this makes no difference to the total number of your rest hours.

A daily rest period is usually 11 uninterrupted hours but can be split into two: first minimum 3 hours, second minimum 9 hours. This means altogether 12 hours' rest. This would not count as a reduction in a daily rest period.

Weekly rest

A week is a period of time between 00.00 Monday and 24.00 Sunday. Weekly rest is generally an uninterrupted period of 45 hours. This can be reduced to 24 hours; however, you are legally required to make up this rest time within three weeks of taking the reduced rest. If, for example, you take a reduced weekly rest period of 24 uninterrupted hours, within three weeks you must take a weekly rest period of 66 uninterrupted hours.

A new weekly rest period commences after six 24-hour periods have elapsed since the last weekly rest period.

Rest taken as compensation for a reduced weekly rest period shall be attached to another rest period of at least 9 hours. The reduction must be compensated for 'en bloc' – it may not be split.

Where a driver chooses to take daily rest and reduced weekly rest periods away from base, these may be taken in the vehicle as long as it has suitable sleeping facilities and the vehicle is stationary.

A weekly rest period which begins in one week and continues into the following week may be attached to either of these weeks.

Drivers' Hours Rules simplified

1   Maximum driving time 9 hours per day. This can be extended to 10 hours twice a week.

2   Take 45-minute break after 4½ hours of driving.

3   The break can be split into 15 minutes, then 30 minutes: not 30 followed by 15. (Over-complicated, much easier to take full 45 minutes.)

4   Park up and take break on or ideally before 4½ hours (1 minute over is illegal).

5   If driving for 10 hours, you will need two 45-minute breaks.

6   If using Digicard VU tachograph machine, be sure to take 46 or 47-minute break (sometimes VU is not accurate enough and will show 45 minutes as 44½ – this now becomes an illegal break and will generate an infringement!).

7   Maximum 6 consecutive shifts in 1 week.

8   Ensure you take 11 hours' rest between end of one shift and start of next. This can be reduced to 9 hours twice a week.

9   Weekly rest period is 45 hours.

10 Maximum driving time in 1 week is 56 hours. If driving 2 consecutive weeks, maximum hours must be 90. (Example: 56 hours 1st week, then 34 hours 2nd week.)

11 If your total driving and working time equals 45 hours or less in 1 week and you then take a rest period of 45 hours or more, you will be totally compliant with drivers' hours rules and working time rules.

12 Maximum total shift duration is 15 hours during the day, 10 hours during the night.

Drivers' Hours Rules tips and advice

1   Make a note of the time you actually start driving.

2   Set alarm on phone for 4 hours on (acts as a reminder and also allows 30 minutes to find a place to park up).

3   When on break remember to alter symbol on VU to rest (bed symbol) then either press down button on VU to see break time or set alarm for 46 minutes, then again make a note of the time you resume driving.

4   Reset alarm for 4 hours on.

5   At any time, if you press down arrow, VU should show exact driving time. (Only records time when the truck wheels are actually turning, not stuck in traffic etc.)

6   New types of VU will flash on 4 hours and 15 minutes as warning to take a break.

7   Remember to take minimum of 30-minute break within 6 hours of starting working, regardless of whether or not you have driven 4½ hours (working time regulation).

Chapter 4
Mock-up of New Driver's Shift

Introduction

These mock shift pages are intended to be of help during the first shift or three. Revision of these pages before starting a new job may be useful – to give reminders and some advice.

The first shift I ever did was on an articulated truck. At the very first drop I managed to smash the passenger side mirror off whilst manoeuvring past a large skip. I ended up with a piece of mirror glass gaffa taped on and a long drive to Plymouth ahead. It certainly wasn't the most relaxing day I've ever had but still I didn't let it unnerve me.

Hopefully your first shift will go a lot better than mine did! However, remember that everyone makes mistakes when first starting out. Don't let this knock your confidence. This chapter should help you be confident that you are as prepared as possible for what awaits you in your first shift. Having a good idea of the structure of a driver's shift before you start will allow for an easier, less stressful transition into this line of work.

Mock-up of new driver's shift

1   Report to transport office. Fill in the paperwork provided (Q&A self-explanatory). Typical questions are: last shift date, start/finish times, POA, rest (calculated from end time of previous shift and new shift start time), driving licence number etc.

2   Office staff will take a photocopy of your licence, CPC card and digicard.

3   Handover of keys, driver's sheets, delivery addresses and hopefully maps and location of truck and trailer.

4   Find truck, switch on ignition, insert digicard into VU. Answer questions by continuously pressing 'OK' or by doing a manual entry. Then change symbol to cross hammers ('other work'). *Now do not move truck for 15 minutes!!* (See Chapter 1 for advice on VU.)

5   Start vehicle checks and paperwork. (See Chapter 5.)

6   Locate and couple up to trailer, do all checks to vehicle and also check load correct and secure. (See Chapters 5 and 7.)

7   Complete paperwork and plan route.

8   Now make a note of the time you actually start driving, then set alarm on phone for 4 hours' time. This acts as a reminder and allows 30 minutes to find a park-up. At any time, if you need to check how much actual driving time has elapsed, just press down arrow on VU. (See Chapter 1.)

9   If you are unable to find truck or trailer, ask the shunter or another driver.

10   Make sure that within 6 hours of putting digicard into VU
     (starting actual work) or within 4½ hours' continuous driving,
     a break is taken – a 45-minute break is required when driving,
     a 30-minute break is required when doing other work. I
     recommend taking a 45-minute break on whichever one of
     these occurs first. (See Chapters 2 and 3.)

11   When on break, remember to alter VU to bed symbol (rest).

Note: If required press 'down' button on VU to see up-to-the-
minute break time taken. I recommend taking a full 46 or
47-minute break.

12   For POA (basically time kept waiting), remember to alter
     symbol on VU.

13   Do all feasible deliveries and keep to all breaks.

14   Return to depot, drop off trailer, do checks and fuel up.

15   Park up truck. Do printout from VU and keep it. Eject card.

16   Hand in all completed paperwork, keys etc. (See Chapter 6.)

17   Office will download digicard.

18   Finish.

19   Make a note in diary of date and start/finish shift times/POA
     and any problems incurred.

20   Be sure to have 11 hours' rest from end of shift to start of
     next shift. Can reduce to 9 hours three times a week.
     (See Chapter 3.)

Note: maximum shift duration is 15 hours for a day shift and 10 hours for a night shift.

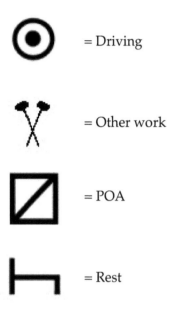

= Driving

= Other work

= POA

= Rest

Shift Check List

The shift check list included in this section is one which I have created and use to help make life a bit easier. I make sure that I have one, attached to a clip board, whilst I am on the job; to act as a task-reminder at the start of my day. It also helps me to keep an eye on my hours during a shift. As the shift progresses, I continue to fill in the sheet with break times, P.O.A. times etc. This helps me to keep track of everything I've done, and everything that I still need to do. In order to make filling it out as clear as possible, I have included a filled in example and a blank example. It's not necessary to use this list, but you my find it helpful to do so.

Note: It's good practice. If on local multi-drop work set phone alarm to 5½ hours (gives 30 minutes warning to find a park up). On long distance work set alarm to 4 hours (gives 30 minutes warning to find a park up).

SHIFT CHECK LIST

- Insert Digi Card, Card Time in = _0=800_

- Manuel Entry, Vehicle Stationary For 15 min (Vehicle Checks).

- Fuel Level = _¾_

- Trailer Height = _14'6_

- Trailer Brake On? _✓_

- BayLight Green? _✓_

- Bridge Tag? _✓_

- Alter satnav / height, weight? _✗_ 14.6/44 tons

- Start Drive (Set Alarm On Phone).

- Start Drive Time = _08:50_

- Drive Break (47mins)

  - After 4½ hrs driving

    - Alter Tacho Symbol – on break

    - Break time = _13.20_ to _14.07_

  - Working Time Directive – Break Must Be Taken After 6 hrs.

- Lock On Dock, Fuel Up.

- Vehicle Checks. Defects?

- Print Out, Take Card Out.

- POA = _45 min_

- Time Sheet.

- End Shift Time = _19.30_

SHIFT CHECK LIST

- Insert Digi Card, Card Time in = _____
- Manuel Entry, Vehicle Stationary For 15 min (Vehicle Checks).
- Fuel Level = _____
- Trailer Height = _____
- Trailer Brake On? ____
- BayLight Green? ____
- Bridge Tag? ____
- Alter satnav / height, weight? ✗___
- Start Drive (Set Alarm On Phone).
- Start Drive Time = _____
- Drive Break (47mins)
  - After 4½ hrs driving
    - Alter Tacho Symbol – on break
    - Break time = _____ to _____
  - Working Time Directive – Break Must Be Taken After 6 hrs.
- Lock On Dock, Fuel Up.
- Vehicle Checks. Defects?
- Print Out, Take Card Out.
- POA = _____
- Time Sheet.
- End Shift Time = _____

Chapter 5

Mandatory Vehicle Inspection Checks

Introduction

This chapter outlines the mandatory vehicle checks which you, as the driver, must carry out. I have also included examples of paperwork and checklists likely to be given to you to fill in. These are quite self-explanatory, but you do need to be quite thorough as you could find yourself blamed for any damage or defects which are overlooked. It can also threaten your licence if any defects are discovered after you have signed the paperwork. This paperwork is legally binding, so be sure not to rush. Only sign it if you're confident that you have been thorough in your checks.

Note: if you are disturbed or distracted whilst completing these checks, or the paperwork, it's advisable to **retrace** previous steps taken before continuing. Remember, it is completely the driver's responsibility once the vehicle hits the road!

Cab Front

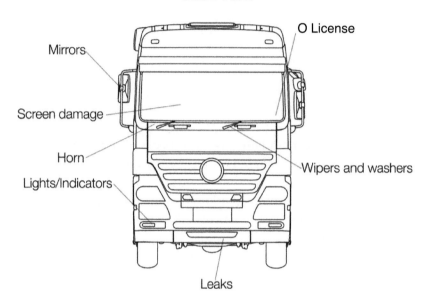

Mirrors

O License

Screen damage

Horn

Lights/Indicators

Wipers and washers

Leaks

Cab Back

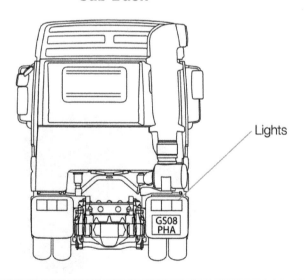

Lights

GS08 PHA

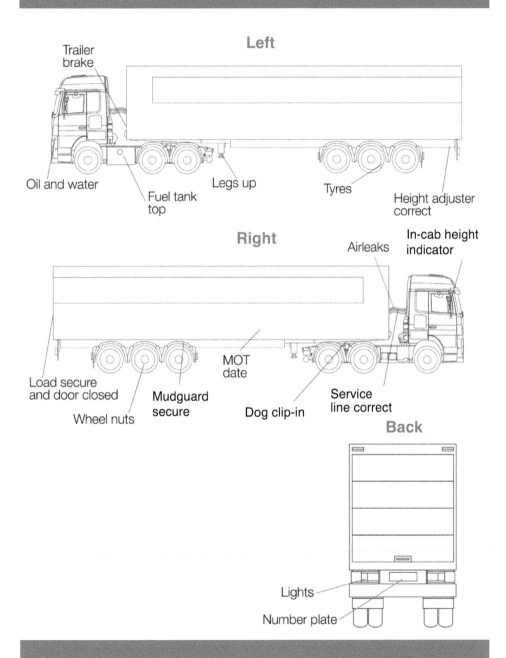

Left

Trailer brake

Oil and water

Legs up

Fuel tank top

Tyres

Height adjuster correct

Right

Airleaks

In-cab height indicator

Load secure and door closed

Wheel nuts

Mudguard secure

MOT date

Dog clip-in

Service line correct

Back

Lights

Number plate

Vehicle Check Sheet 1

Fill each box with a '☑' if the condition is satisfactory
or a '☒' if there is a defect.

TRUCK CHECK	JOURNEY	
	BEFORE	AFTER
Brake lines and coupling – present in good working order		
Fuel cap and seal – present free from leaks		
Levels & leaks – engine oil, water, fuel, AdBlue		
Lights – operational, in good working order		
MOT disc – valid, clearly displayed		
Road fund & O licence discs – valid, clearly displayed		
Tyres – inflation, tread depth, in good working order		
Wings, mudguards and spray suppression equipment – satisfactory condition and secure		
Excessive engine exhaust smoke – visual check		
Indicators – in good working order		
Mirrors – presentable, in good working order		
Service week sticker – valid, displayed – number to be written		
Wheels – satisfactory condition, fixings secure		
Wipers & washers – satisfactory condition, in good working order		
Digital tachograph fitted – spare print roll present		
Horn – in good working order		
Seating – satisfactory condition & secure		
Air leaks – listen for leaks		
Glass & windscreen – presentable, good condition, free from obstruction		
In-cab height indicator – present and correctly set		
Seat belt – in good working order		

Vehicle Check Sheet 2

Fill each box with a '☑' if the condition is satisfactory
or a '☒' if there is a defect.

TRAILER CHECK	JOURNEY	
	BEFORE	AFTER
Rear door shutter – in good working order		
Reflectors – free from damage		
Service week sticker – valid, clearly displayed – number to be written		
Tyres – inflation, tread depth, damage		
Wheels – satisfactory and secure		
Wings, mudguards and spray suppression equipment – satisfactory condition and secure		
Indicators – in good working order		
Landing legs warning device – in good working order		
Marker boards – satisfactory condition, free from damage		
Lights – in good working order, free from damage		
Mavis rail – operational		
Load security restraint in place – 2 bars/straps at rear		
MOT disc – valid, displayed – MOT month to be written		
Number plate satisfactory condition, and secure		
Park brake operational/air leaks – aural check		

Service week numbers

If the company you are working for require the service
numbers of the truck, trailer, or both to be added to the
checks sheets. They are usually to be found on the back
of the cab (artic tractor unit).On the outside of the bulk
head or side of (trailer). Cab door or side of body
(rigid).

Chapter 6
Coupling Procedures

Introduction

This chapter shows the various scenarios to do with coupling and uncoupling. The diagrams show some of the problems that can be encountered if you are not on your game. It's quite a straightforward procedure; however, make sure that you do not let time constraints pressure you into feeling rushed or distracted. This is where mistakes happen. Take enough time to carry out this task properly. If you do get distracted, by someone or something, make sure you **retrace** previous steps before proceeding.

Artic Coupling Procedure (split)

a. Reverse up to the trailer, handbrake on, check trailer brake is on (pulled out), fifth wheel bar (handle) pulled out. **Is the trailer height correct?**

b. Reverse halfway under the trailer – handbrake on, connect service lines – airline.

c. Reverse under until pin locks in.

d. Select first gear and tug trailer twice.

e. Handbrake on, fit fifth wheel clip (dog clip).

f. Trailer brake off.

g. Wind up legs.

h. Fit number plate.

Artic Coupling Procedure (close)

a. Reverse up to trailer, handbrake on, check trailer brake is on, fifth wheel bar pulled out. **Is the trailer height correct?** (If Mavis rail fitted slide it all the way across.)

b. Reverse under the trailer until the pin locks in.

c. Select first gear, tug trailer twice.

d. Handbrake on, fit dog clip.

e. Fit service/airlines.

f. Trailer brake off.

g. Wind up legs.

h. Fit number plate.

Artic Uncoupling Procedure

a. Handbrake on.

b. Trailer brake on.

c. Wind legs down.

d. Service/airlines disconnected.

e. Remove number plate.

f. Pull fifth wheel locking lever out (unlocked position).

g. Double-check all procedures.

h. Drive out.

Example of missing the pin due to deflated suspension airbags.

King pin release handle and dog clip.

Airlines and Service lines.

Considerations during coupling

If the trailer is at an incorrect height, use the handheld suspension unit to raise or lower the truck to match the trailer height.

If you are still unsure if the trailer is too high, you can reverse under most of the way, raise the truck up until you feel the weight of the trailer and then reverse the last few inches until the pin locks in.

Note: Some companies do not allow split coupling. Always check with each company transport office.

Always, always check trailer brake is on! Once you fit the airline the brakes will automatically release. During split coupling, there is an extreme danger of the trailer rolling forward, if the yard is on a downwards incline, and of you therefore being crushed between it and the cab.

The object of the tug test is to ensure that the pin is locked in. Give the trailer two strong tugs but do not drag it forward as this will risk damage to the legs etc.

Mavis rail (Montracon articulated vehicle interconnection system): This modern technology is fitted on newer trailers. It is located on the bulkhead (front of trailer). It allows the service lines and airlines to be connected from the ground without having to climb onto the back of the truck. Pull one or two levers (pins) and the whole rail slides out.

    a.   Make sure to lock it back into its original position when you are finished, or it could slide out whilst travelling down the road.

    b.   Be very careful of other traffic whilst using it, because **you will have your back to any possible danger!!!**

Bad coupling example A shows a trailer which is too high, therefore missing the pin. This will result in damage to the rear of the cab and to the trailer bulkhead.

Bad coupling example B shows a trailer which is too low. This will cause damage to rear lights and mudguards.

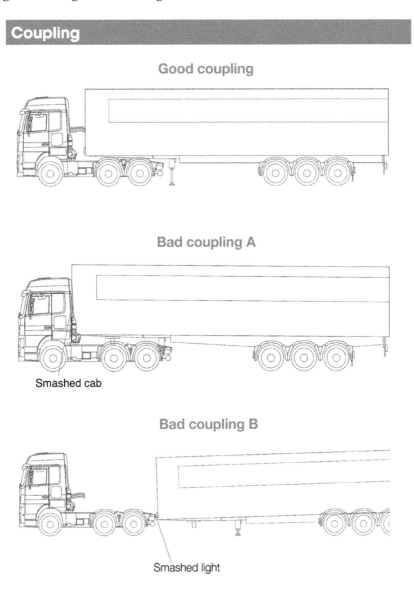

Coupling

Good coupling

Bad coupling A

Smashed cab

Bad coupling B

Smashed light

Chapter 7
Loading and Unloading

Introduction

The aim of this chapter is to help you gain an understanding of safe loading and unloading. With regard to loading/unloading equipment, I have outlined the safe use and carriage of roller cages and pallets, and essential tips for the use of pump trucks. I have also included pictures and a description of how to use height adjusters and tail lifts, and a list of considerations to keep in mind whilst you are loading/unloading.

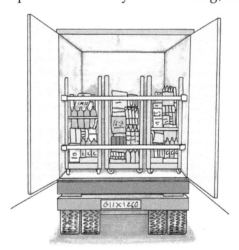

Useful you tube videos:

Tail lift operation

S and E Logistics

https://www.youtube.com/watch?v=butf9ThPBBU

Alan White

https://www.youtube.com/watch?v=3ahQLLKeUuQ

Roller cages

In the event of a full load of roller cages, you need to have at least a minimum of 2 load restraining bars, one top, one bottom which are spaced out evenly every 5 rows. If rollers are very heavy, i.e. containing drinks, tins, etc., you will need 2 bars every 3 rows – pallets require 2 bars or straps every 3 to 4 rows.

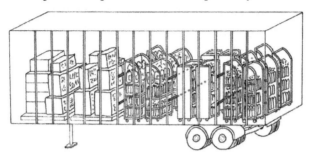

When unloading on an incline, always level the vehicle by raising or lowering the suspension on the truck or trailer or both. On a steep uphill incline (Artic) raising the tractor unit up and also lowering the trailer down may be required to achieve a level load. Follow the opposite procedure for downhill inclines. **Never** remove straps or bars if the vehicle is not level. Each roller could easily weigh up to 500kg each. This system applies to both artic and rigid trucks.

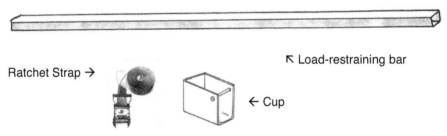

Ratchet Strap →

↖ Load-restraining bar

← Cup

Bars and cups

The cups lock into rails fitted to the sidewall of the trailer. The 2 cups are slightly different, one is a fixed unit and the other has a lift up catch. Very easy to use, just fit the bar into fixed unit cup, then put the other end into the adjustable cup. (Fit snug against the load)

Ratchel straps

To adjust length prior to attaching or to undo a tightened strap. Pull clip back, then, snap handle back as far as it will go until unlocks, releases and fully opens out. To tighten, close then use the ratchet handle. (Avoid twisting the strap).

Roller cages

Note: Extreme danger to you and others! The restraining bars could potentially be holding back 3 rows. i.e. 9 rollers! If one or more rows start to move you **will** not stop them! You could be crushed in the corner of the trailer or the roller cage might fall off the back and potentially hit somebody.

When manual handling full cages, always push or pull. Do not walk alongside them, if a wheel brakes there is high risk of injury.

Empty rollers are designed to be easily folded up and to slot inside one another. Usual loading practice is to start at the front of the trailer, create 3 even forward facing rows.

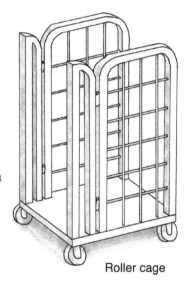

Roller cage

Then fit 2 securing bars halfway along the rows and at the end of the rows.

Pump trucks

A pump truck acts as a manual version of a forklift. Its main purpose is for loading and unloading pallets of goods. Pump the handle backwards and forwards to lift up the pallets. Press the handle/lever to lower.

If using one inside a trailer, you must ensure the vehicle is level! A pallet can easily weigh up to 10 times a person's body weight. It can run away as you give chase down the trailer. Pump trucks don't usually have brakes; the only way to stop them is by lowering the pallet. Just remember to take it slow until you get used to using one.

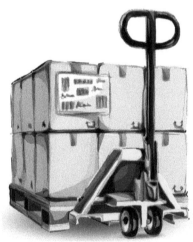

Note: pallets are usually rectangular. They need to be the correct way round to fit 2 side-by-side on a trailer.

Take care not to trap your feet under the wheels or pallet, or hands between pump truck handle and trailer side.

Trailer height adjuster

Located near passenger-side rear corner. Usually push it inwards and rotate lever left or right to lower or raise; pull it back out until it clicks and it should self-level the trailer to correct height.

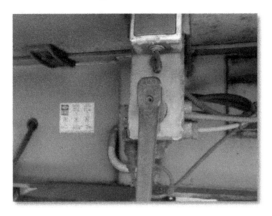

Truck height adjuster

This is located either behind the driver's seat or on the side of the seat. The adjuster is simple to use.

Usually press centre of switch until it illuminates, then press function arrows to raise or lower. Press centre of switch again for vehicle to self level (return to normal operating height). When adjusting suspension height, either leave control pad on seat or write note to self and put it on dashboard. This acts as a reminder to prevent forgetting and driving away with the suspension airbags over or under inflated. Driving away in the wrong position can cause damage to tyres or suspension airbags.

Tail lift operation

Some trucks have an isolator switch in the cab. This needs to be in the 'on' position to operate the tail lift. Switches and buttons are usually found on the near side of the trailer; there are usually more buttons inside the trailer (near side just inside the trailer). A little lever clip will need to be pushed or pulled to unfold the lift.

Warning: whilst raising the lift, there is a serious risk of crushing your toes if you get them trapped between the lift and the trailer floor. Also, **never ever insert your hands and try to free an underslung tail lift if it jams!** If it suddenly moves it will turn your hands into marmalade. Instead, get help or walk away.

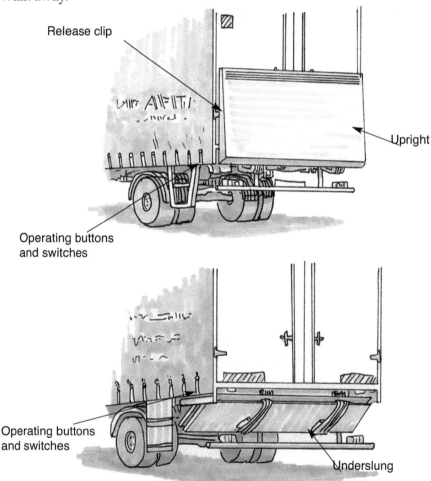

Release clip

Upright

Operating buttons and switches

Operating buttons and switches

Underslung

Loading and unloading considerations

1. Need sidelights switched on in truck in order to be able to work interior trailer lights.

2. When unloading or loading or carrying out checks etc. change VU symbol to 'other work' (cross hammers).

3. If you are kept waiting to be loaded or unloaded, change the symbol to 'POA' (supposed to be waiting time known in advance, not always the case). When you drive away, usually the VU symbol will automatically change itself to the driving symbol.

4. Load safety tips – always check the load yourself and always make sure it is fully secure. **Never** trust that someone else has chained, strapped or barred up the load properly. The loaders could have changed shift halfway, been distracted, been short of equipment or not cared!

5. **Important:** try not to be hurried when completing the task of loading/unloading. Your safety comes first, the load second. Also, if for any reason you have to move the truck halfway through, keep calm and collected. Remember, you are in the middle of a process, so **retrace** previous steps if you need to. Always, always **re-secure** the load before moving!

Chapter 8
Load Chaining and Lashing

Introduction

This chapter contains information on load safety, personal safety, mandatory regulations and how to use the different types of securing equipment.

The three main types of load securement

Fully contained

Cargo must not be able to shift or tip and must be restrained from sideways movement either by the vehicle structure or sideways movement.

Secured cages

Suspension highered

Under slung tail lift

Tail lift controls

Suspension lowered

Standard tail lift

Load holding plates

Ratchet strap

Immobilized

The cargo can be immobilized by structures or a combination of structure, blocking and bracing.

Secured on vehicle

The cargo must be secured by tie downs and can be accompanied by blocking, bracing, friction mats, other cargo, dunnage or a combination of these.

Equipment

Each load will have its own securement specifications. Know what they are:

- The load rating of the trailer

- The weight of equipment being moved

- The load rating of chains, straps and binders. These ratings can be found on the equipment by means of a stamp, a fitted tag or in the accompanying manuals.

WLL – working load limits

Each piece of equipment has a WLL. Here is a guide for the most commonly used transportation chain and straps.

Chains

The most common high grade 70, 3/8th chain is rated for 6600 pounds securement value if the markings found on it are 7. Could be 7, rg 7, L 7, 70 etc. This indicates it's a genuine type 70 chain. If there are no markings the chain should be automatically down rated.

Always check chains are in good condition and have not been mended in the past. Things to look out for are stretched, bent or twisted links and welded or added lap or quick links. Any of the above make the chains void for use.

Straps

High quality WLL marked or tagged 3 inch straps have a working load limit of 3000 pounds.

High quality WLL marked or tagged 4 inch straps have a working load limit of 4000 pounds.

Some higher quality straps can exceed these limits.

Check for damage; rips, tares, holes. There should be little to none.

Example of best practise load strapping/lashing

The number of lashings required depends on:

Weight of load / shape of Load / whether the load is placed against the head board of the trailer / ratings of lashings / friction between load and load bed of the trailer / how many load securing tensioners are used / angle of lashing (ideally set lashings as vertical as possible).

Cross chaining, regulations and best practise for securing machinery

Heavy equipment must have a minimum of four tie downs. Any appendages require an extra tie down.

There are two types of chain tighteners in use. Ratchet binder and a lever binder. These are also WLL rated and will be stamped with the working load limits.

Procedure chaining:

Find flat level ground

1) Load machinery

2) Unscrew ratchet binders full out

3) Attach chains, pull tight

4) If machine has manufacturers tie down points (eyelets), chain to these.

5) Set chains, two facing front, two facing back (creating opposite forward backward forces) set them on roughly 45 degree angles (creating down force) and prevents machinery from movement, up, down, left, right, forwards and backwards.

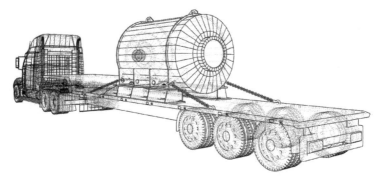

6) Attach binders and tighten chains evenly until taut.

7) Store any remainder of chain by wrapping it around binders.

Note

Machinery with tyres are more difficult to secure tightly and likely to bounce slightly in transit loosening chains. Check this type of load more often and be aware of slow punctures letting tyres down thus loosening chains.

Beware of hydraulics. Hydraulics tend to creep down. Never get under raised hydraulics or in any tight space where machinery could creep, trap and potentially crush you to death.

Secure ratchet binders in fixed position to guard against them undoing in transit.

Chapter 9
Manoeuvring

Introduction

The aim of this chapter is to show you the recommended positioning techniques to aid the manoeuvring of vehicles onto bays in busy yards. 2 types of scenario will be focused on:

- Manoeuvring in a spacious yard.

- Manoeuvring in a tight yard.

You should find this information useful, as you never know how much space you will be given. With practise, manoeuvring becomes much easier.

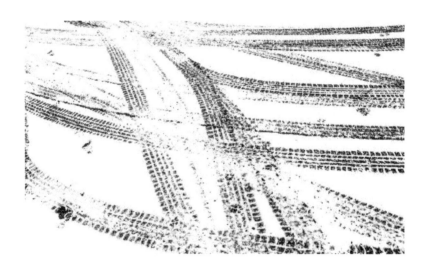

Manoeuvring

Spacious yard

If yard protocol allows, approach the bays offside on. Drive along the rank until you reach the required bay. Swing the truck up towards the opposite row of bays. The idea here is to leave the rear of the trailer positioned towards the intended bay, as it makes it easier for reversing in.

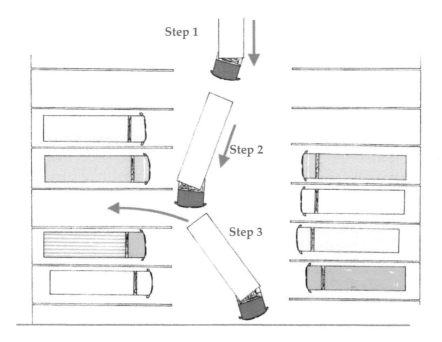

Tight (small) yard

You need a different approach for a tight yard. Ideally, you should aim to be offside on and centrally positioned. Line up the back of the trailer with the intended bay, then jack-knife the trailer 180 degrees onto the bay.

Note) In tight yards, this manoeuvre is very difficult until you get the hang of it, to avoid causing damage. If you need help, **ask!** If you find the yard folk are not very friendly, you could offer a cash incentive in exchange for assistance, such as a fiver. (Shame on any man who takes it rather than helping for free!!).

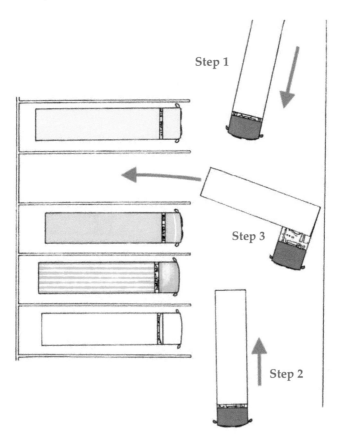

Chapter **10**
Key Safe (Lock on Dock)

Introduction

This chapter focuses on the key safe procedure. This system was designed to prevent accidents and injuries. In the past, there were a lot of incidents of trucks pulling off bays whilst loading or unloading was still taking place. This resulted in many injuries to loaders, some serious. For example forklifts and pump trucks came crashing down off the docks.

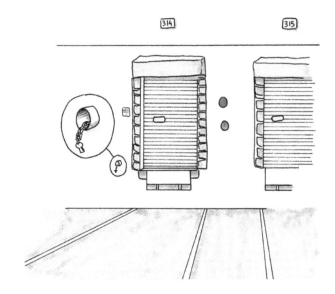

Here are a few scenarios of why, in the past, drivers have prematurely driven off:

1. The driver fell asleep and woke up after some time to find that all was quiet. He/she checked the time. Half asleep, he/she believed that loading/unloading must have finished and so drove off.

2. The driver could hear that loading was underway. He/she was under pressure to get to the next destination and therefore a bit distracted. After a while, all went quiet. Not thinking clearly, he/she believed that loading/unloading had finished. Perhaps, due to past experience, he/she thought that there had been a change of shift in the warehouse and that the previous loader must have forgotten to change the bay light to green. He/she therefore drove off.

Please be aware that not all yards use the key safe procedure. In these situations, it is good to keep these scenarios above in mind whilst loading/unloading is taking place.

Key safe (lock on dock) procedure

<u>Artic (class 1), rigid (class 2)</u>

The usual procedure is to put the ignition keys onto a chain. The warehouse staff will pull them up and keep hold of them until the truck is loaded. Keep an eye on the mirror; on completion the bay light will change to green and the keys will be dropped.

On the rare occasion that the keys are either hanging on the chain or in the truck, but the bay light is still on red:

- Go and speak to warehouse staff.

- Check all is fine.

- Get bay light changed to green.

- Drive off.

- **Never** ever drive off on a red bay light!

Artic (Class 1)

Picking up trailers

- Check bay light on green.

- Reverse up to trailer.

- Fetch key from hook/chain next to building.

- Undo lock on airline (trailer).

- Put key and lock back on hook/chain. Commence coupling up to trailer.

Dropping trailers

- Reverse trailer safely into empty bay.

- Uncouple truck from trailer.

- Fetch key and lock from hook/chain next to building.

- Secure lock to airline on trailer.

- Return key.

- Press button to change bay light to red.

Safety tips

a. Always check bay light on green before attempting to couple up.

b. Never reverse under trailer on red bay light.

Note: don't forget to remove trailer number plate.

Chapter **11**
Refrigerated Trailers and Tautliners

Introduction

Please find, in this chapter, a thorough guide to using two of the most commonly used trailers – refrigerated and tautliner trailers. The same, or very similar, steps also apply to Class 2 rigid trucks. Technology on trucks is ever-changing; however, all are basically similar to operate.

Note: New curtain side trailers now have safe working load restraining information written on to the actual curtain.

Useful you tube videos:

Refrigeration Trailers – ProperOperation fftitrans

https://www.youtube.com/watch?v=vBXH76zpXCI&t=226s

Wickes IW Curtainsider V4 Bob Weaver Published on Nov 22

https://www.youtube.com/watch?v=OG4JgFD8PNo&t=595s

Fuel Tank and Gauge

User's Guide to Refrigerated Trailers

Typically, the transporting temperature for ambient and chilled loads is +3°C, and, for frozen loads, the transporting temperature is -20°C.

Usually there are movable drop-down curtains inside the trailer to create two separate compartments; this makes it possible to have both an ambient and a frozen load in one trailer.

Operation

1. Flick the switch marked 'start/run' from 'off' to 'start/run'. Wait a few seconds; an alarm will sound, then the fridge will start up.

2. Use the switch/button marked '1/2' to select compartment 1/2, then press up/down arrows to alter the temperature and press '=' button to confirm.

The red diesel (gas oil) fuel tank is underslung beneath the trailer. The fuel gauge is located on the side of the tank. Always check that the cap is tight and that the rubber seal is intact. One third to half a tank of fuel should usually see out a 10-hour shift.

Tri-axle fridge trailer:

Adjustable curtains:

User's Guide to Tautliners

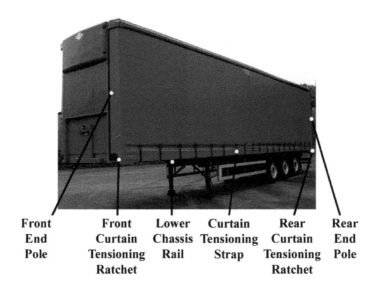

Front End Pole	Front Curtain Tensioning Ratchet	Lower Chassis Rail	Curtain Tensioning Strap	Rear Curtain Tensioning Ratchet	Rear End Pole

Curtain tensioning strap. In this example, the strap is in the closed tense position. To release strap, lift lever [a], pull the rear strap down and unhook hook [b] from lower chassis rail.

To secure the strap, pull the hook [b] under the lower chassis rail and secure to rail. Then pull down on the upper strap until taut and then pull down lever [a] until it clips into place.

Typical corner tensioning ratchet. To release push handle firmly inwards. To tension, pull handle forwards and backward until the curtain is tight.

How to open the curtains:

Release the curtain tensioning straps, as described above, to the extent you need to open the curtain. Next release the corner tensioning ratchet and pull out the curtain attached to the corner pole. Push the pole upwards until the bottom of the pole is free of the ratchet and pull outward. Lower the pole until it is free of the top securing pin. Pull the curtain back in the required direction.

Curtain	Central
Slide	Slide Rail
Rail	Support Bar

Warning:

Never take out both corner poles at the same time; you risk pulling the curtain off the curtain rail and it is very difficult to re-attach.

How to close the curtains:

Pull the curtain closed and lift the top of the corner pole up until it is located in the top securing pin, hold it up and locate the bottom of the pole onto ratchet. Use the ratchet to tension the curtain and then do up the curtain straps as described on the preceding page.

Safety:

When it is windy the curtains, strap hooks and in particular the corner pole can flap about uncontrollably. This can result in serious injury or damage. To prevent this it is advisable to only open the curtains to the minimum required. Also it is advisable to pull the hooks up to release lever and use the curtain strap nearest the curtain pole to clip it into place on either the lower chassis rail or one of the tensioned straps.

Chapter **12**
Gearboxes

Introduction

Shown in this chapter are various types of gearboxes. I have chosen to focus on the most commonly found gearboxes in the industry today. Diagrams and descriptions of how to use each model are included.

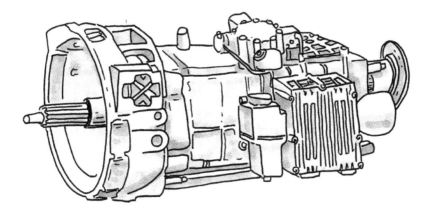

This is an example of a modern automatic gear box gear selector.

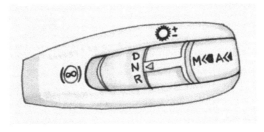

A is for fully automatic mode/M is for manual gear selection mode. D=drive/R=reverse/N=neutral. To operate, hold down the foot brake then select the appropriate gear.

A – Range Change

This is essentially a 16-speed gearbox – 4 gears in a low range, 4 gears in a

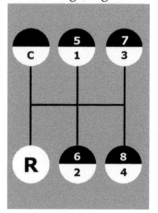

high range and a splitter (overdrive) which allows for half-gears. 'C' stands for 'crawler gear', which is useful for very steep inclines.

Go through gears 1 to 4, pull up the switch on the front of the stick. To access gears 5-8, use the other switch for splitter gears.

B – Range Change (SCANIA)

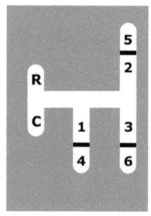

This box is fitted to SCANIA trucks. It is basically the same as example A; the only difference is that it only contains 3 gears in a low range and 3 gears in a high range.

C – Splitter

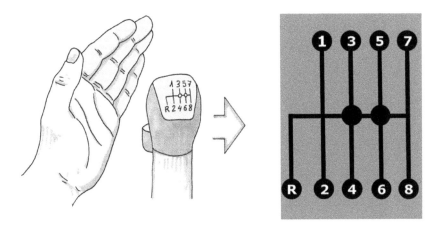

A splitter box is a 16-speed gearbox. Go through gears 1-4, then pull the stick sideways towards the driver's seat to change the range and access gears 5–8. It should be obvious when you are changing range – feel the resistance through the stick. The switch on the side is for half-gears (overdrive).

D – Automatic

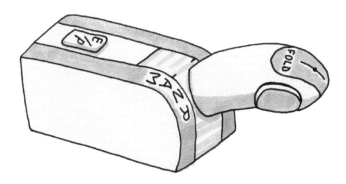

In this example of an automatic gearbox, select 'A' for full-automatic mode. Select 'M' to drive in manual mode. When in manual mode, use the switches on the side of the stick to change gear.

Chapter 13
Roping and Sheeting

Introduction

Explained below are the basics for the roping and sheeting of an open load.

Note) it is necessary that, prior to attempting this task, you undergo full training in the exact placing of sheets, straps and ropes, and in the tying of the various knots used. Rest assured, you won't be expected to attempt any of these procedures until you have been shown by a professional.

Example A - Ropes not tight enough, tensioned unevenly:

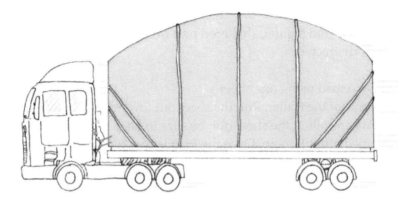

Example B - Sheets placed in wrong order:

Roping and Sheeting

The basic principles of roping and sheeting are as follows:

Ideally, you should find a quiet, sheltered part of the yard where you won't be disturbed or distracted.

To secure down a load using one sheet –
Start at either end of the trailer. Roll the sheet out towards the opposite end of the trailer. When rolling the sheet out, be sure to keep it taught and to expel any trapped air as you go. Once the load is covered, secure all ropes and/or straps tightly, making sure they're all evenly tensioned.

To secure down a load using two sheets –
Start at the rear end of the trailer. Attach the first sheet over the rear end of the trailer, then attach the second sheet over the front end of the trailer. Make sure that the front sheet overlaps with the rear sheet (this stops the wind from getting underneath the rear sheet, which could loosten it and cause it to start to lift it whilst in transit).

Note) In windy conditions, you should only roll your sheeting out a little bit at a time and secure as you go.

Please take the time to note the following **dangers:**

- Walking on top of a load that's unstable and could move.

- Walking on top of a load which has an unsecured sheet, as there is a possibility of you falling down into a space in between the load.

- Being blown off the top of the load when the wind lifts the unsecured sheet.

- The load coming loose, shifting, falling off the trailer.

Chapter **14**

Maximum Vehicle Laden Weights

Introduction

Included below is a useful but not uncomplicated table regarding the legal maximum vehicle laden (gross) weights of various goods vehicles. It was produced by the Department of Transport in 2003, for the use of Magistrates when presiding over cases of overloading. Since this is the information magistrates use when deciding whether or not a particular goods vehicle was overloaded, you can't go too far wrong if you abide by the weights on this table.

A Simplified Guide To Lorry Types And Weights

Recommended Description			Identifier	UK Maximum Gross Weight (tonnes)	Shape
LIGHT GOODS VEHICLES			2 axles	3.5	no rear side windows
L **O** **R** **R** **I** **E** **S**		SMALLER 2-AXLE LORRIES	2 axles	Over 3.5 7.5	
		BIGGER 2-AXLE LORRIES	2 axles	Over 7.5 18	
	HEAVY		3 axles rigid	25 26*	
			3 axles artic.	26	
	GOODS	MULTI-	4 axles rigid	30 32*	
	VEHICLES		4 axles artic.	36 38*	
	(Vehicles over 7.5 tonnes gross require a Heavy Goods Vehicle Driver's Licence)		Vehicle and draw-bar trailer 4 axles	30 36**	
		AXLE	5 axles or more artic. See note (a)	40	
			Vehicle and draw-bar trailer 5 axles See note (a)	40**	
		LORRIES	6 axles artic. See note (b)	41*	
			6 axles draw-bar See note (b)	41* and **	
			5 or 6 axles artic. See notes (b) and (c)	44* and ***	
			6 axles draw-bar	44*,** and ***	
			6 axles artic. See note (b) and (d)	44*	
			6 axles draw-bar See note (b) and (d)	44* and **	

*	If the driving axle is not a steering axle, has twin tyres and road friendly suspension, or if each driving axle is fitted with twin tyres and the maximum weight for each axle does not exceed 8.55 tonnes.

**	Distance between the rear axle of the motor vehicle and the front axle of the trailer is not less than 3 metres.

***	If the vehicle is being used for combined transport.

(a)	5 axles or more artic and the 5 axles or more drawbar could alternatively have a 3 axle motor vehicle and a 2 axle trailer.

(b)	Conditions:

- each vehicle must have at least 3 axles.

- drive axle has twin tyre and road friendly suspension and maximum of 10.5 tonnes, or each driving axle is fitted with twin tyres and has a maximum of 8.5 tonnes.

- trailer has road friendly suspension.

(c)	Conditions for operation on 5 axles:

- must have 3 axles on tractor unit.

- single container 40ft in length (conforming to standards laid down by the International Standards Organisation) being carried only.

- vehicle being used for international journey.

(d)	Powered by a low pollution engine.

Maximum Vehicle Laden Weights

For the purposes of full disclosure, please note that under UK law, there are two sets of regulations concerning maximum vehicle laden (gross) weights, which a company can choose to abide by:

1. The Authorised Weight Regulations 1998.

2. The Road Vehicles (Construction and Use) Regulations 1986.

Companies can abide by either set of regulations, but not a combination of the two. For this reason, I suggest that you check with the company that you are working for, as to what the laden (gross) weights of their vehicles are, before you take any of them out on the road.

Added regulations/DVSA up dated drivers rest rules 2018. Source: Vehicle enforcement data for Great Britain

The rules have changed since the 5th of March 2018 so that now lorry, bus and coach drivers who drive tired can be fined for every time they've done so in the last 28 days.

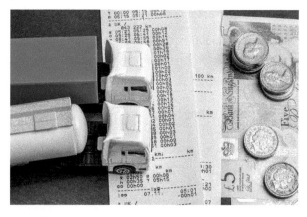

Source – Department of Transport – 'A Simplified Guide to Lorry Types and Weights' – 2003.

Used in accordance with the Open Government Licence for public sector information:

http://www.nationalarchives.gov.uk/doc/open-government-licence/version/3/

If you drive a lorry, bus or coach, you must follow rules on how many hours you can drive and the breaks you need to take.

The Driver and Vehicle Standards Agency (DVSA) can fine drivers up to £300 if they're caught breaking the rules. They can also be prosecuted or have their vehicle immobilised.

Previously , DVSA could only fine drivers for:

- offences committed that day

- ongoing offences, like manipulating tachograph records, which record drivers' hours

Drivers can now be fined for older offences

From Monday 5 March 2018, DVSA traffic examiners started issuing on-the-spot fines for any drivers' hours offences committed in the last 28 days.

In a single roadside check, DVSA traffic examiners can issue fines for up to 5 drivers' hours offences. It means you could be fined up to £1,500 in a single check if you've consistently broken the rules.

It doesn't matter if the offences took place in Great Britain or elsewhere.

The rules will also apply to drivers who don't live in Great Britain. However, they'll need to pay any fines immediately, before being allowed to continue their journey. DVSA will immobilise their vehicle until they pay.

Fines to deter drivers from not resting properly

As well as giving fines to drivers for recent offences, DVSA traffic examiners have started issuing fines to deal with drivers who don't properly rest.

Lorry, bus and coach drivers must take a 45-hour rest break at least every fortnight.

Since 1 November 2017, DVSA has started to fine drivers up to £300 if they spend their (full weekly rest break) in their vehicle in places where it causes a problem. For example, if a lorry driver spends their full break in the cab of their lorry in a layby.

Illegal parking, noise and litter nuisance.

Spending the weekly rest break in the cab can:

- contribute to drivers not properly resting

- expose drivers to poor living conditions

It can also cause problems in local communities. In some areas, lorry drivers have parked illegally or inappropriately while taking the 45-hour break, and have caused residents to complain about noise, litter and anti-social behaviour.

During 2016, authorities in Kent took action against 3,700 lorry drivers for parking illegally or inappropriately.

Targeting problem areas

DVSA traffic examiners target places where this is causing the biggest problems, such as residential areas and laybys.

DVSA will also work with its counterparts in other countries to deal with overseas operators whose drivers regularly do this.

Devastating consequences of driving tired

Crashes involving tired lorry drivers can be devastating. Almost a quarter of injuries in accidents involving lorries are fatal or serious.

About 40% of sleep-related accidents involve commercial vehicles.

According to the Royal Society for the Prevention of Accidents (ROSPA), driving while tired may be responsible for:

- 1 in 5 of all accidents

- up to a quarter of serious and fatal crashes

6,300 drivers' hours fines were given to lorry drivers by DVSA between April 2015 and March 2016.

Source: Vehicle enforcement data for Great Britain.

Chapter 15
Environmentally Friendly - Fuel Saving - Driving

Introduction

Featured here are tips and techniques to drive a truck economically.

Nowadays, companies are very keen on this topic. This is hardly surprising, considering the price of fuel and the fact that an average fully loaded 44 ton truck burns through a gallon of diesel every 6–9 miles. Companies are, therefore, looking to all options to increase miles per gallon.

Note) In a successful attempt to cut costs, some larger companies (such as supermarkets) are now removing one of the two fitted fuel tanks and replacing it with a gas tank. Their trucks would then run on duel fuel, which lowers fuel costs.

Eco-driving

The following set of tips will help you to save as much fuel as possible:

- Avoid unnecessary idling in cold weather if waiting to be loaded/unloaded. Switch off the engine and use night (cab) heater.

- Adjust your driving style to one of forward thinking and anticipation. By reading the road ahead, it can be possible to see obstacles and hazards before reaching them; thus avoiding a lot of heavy braking and accelerating (keeping up momentum).

- Approach traffic lights gradually, avoiding (where possible) coming to a complete stop.

- Set your air deflector to correct height and angle.

- Change gear in the middle of the rev range.

- Check and correct all tyre pressures.

- Avoid speeding.

- Pull sheets/curtains on the trailer tight.

Regen

New fuel efficient trucks have a regen feature. Every so often the system needs particulates such as soot etc cleared out. When the time is due, a sign or signs will appear on the dashboard. Full "how to" directions for this procedure should be found inside the cab .Obviously when clearing the system park a safe distance away from other vehicles.

Chapter **16**
Regulations on Tachograph Exempted Vehicles

(Courtesy of DVSA Document Rules on drivers hours and tachographs. Goods vehicles in GB and Europe.)

This chapter identifies and goes into the regulations on different types of vehicles that do not have to use tachographs.

UK Domestic rules

The UK domestic rules, as contained in the Transport Act 1968, apply to most goods vehicles that are exempt from the EU rules. Separate rules apply to Northern Ireland.

Domestic rules exemptions

The following groups are exempt from the domestic drivers' hours rules:

- drivers of vehicles used by the Armed Forces, the police and fire brigade;

- drivers who always drive off the public road system; and

- private driving, i.e. not in connection with a job or in any way to earn a living.

Domestic driving limits

Driving is defined as being at the controls of a vehicle for the purposes of controlling its movement, whether it is moving or stationary with the engine running, even for a short period of time.

Daily driving
In any working day the maximum amount of driving permitted is **10 hours.** The daily driving limit applies to driving on and off the public road. Off-road driving for the purposes of agriculture, quarrying, forestry, building work or civil engineering counts as duty rather than driving time.

Day:
The day is the 24-hour period beginning with the start of duty time.

Daily duty
In any working day the maximum amount of duty permitted is **11 hours.**

A driver is exempt from the daily duty limit (11 hours) on any working day when he does not drive.

A driver who does not drive for more than 4 hours on each day of the week is exempt from the daily duty limit.

Duty
In the case of an employee driver, this means being on duty (whether driving or otherwise)for anyone who employs him as a driver. This includes all periods of work and driving, but does not include rest or breaks. Employers should also remember that they have additional obligations to ensure that drivers receive adequate rest under health and safety legislation.

For owner drivers, this means driving a vehicle connected with their business, or doing any other work connected with the vehicle and its load.

Drivers of certain vehicles are exempt from the duty but not the driving limit, namely – goods vehicles, including dual purpose vehicles, not exceeding a maximum permitted gross weight of 3.5tonnes,when used:

- by doctors, dentists, nurses, midwives or vets;

- for any service of inspection, cleaning, maintenance, repair, installation or fitting;

- by commercial travellers;

- by the AA, RAC or RSAC; and

- for cinematography or radio and television broadcasting.

The EU rules grant member states the power to apply derogations to further specific categories of vehicles and drivers while on national journeys. The following derogations have been implemented in the UK.

Note: In some cases it may be necessary to refer to case law for definitive interpretations.

Derogations

Vehicles used in connection with sewerage, flood protection, water, gas and electricity maintenance services, road maintenance or control, door-to-door, household refuse collection or disposal, telegraph or telephone services, radio or television broadcasting and the detection of radio or television transmitters or receiver.

Specialised vehicles transporting circus and funfair equipment.

Vehicles used for milk collection from farms or the return to farms of milk containers or milk products intended for animal feed.

Vehicles used exclusively on roads inside hub facilities such as ports, airports, interports and railway terminals.

Notes re: Vehicle exemptions

There have been a number of significant court rulings from the European Court of Justice and British courts dealing with this exemption. Common themes have included a direct and close involvement in the exempt activity;

the principle of a general service in the public interest; and the limited and secondary nature of the transport activity.

It is our view that vehicles used in connection with sewerage, flood protection, water, gas and electricity services must be involved in the maintenance of an existing service (rather than the construction of a new service) to claim the concession.

The types of refuse collection and disposal operations likely to be exempt are: the door-to-door collection of black bin bags, green waste, newspapers or glass from households; the collection of sofas and household appliances from households within a local area; and the clearing of a home following a bereavement, provided refuse collection and disposal is the core purpose.

In addition, the following vehicles are exempt from the EU rules in GB after the European Commission granted a special authorisation:

- any vehicle which is being used by the Royal National Lifeboat Institution;

- any vehicle that was manufactured before 1 January 1947; and

- any vehicle that is propelled by steam.

If it is exempt from the EU rules due to the provisions listed above then the vehicle will usually be in scope of the GB domestic rules when travelling in GB.

In addition to the derogations listed above, there is also a concession in place from the daily and weekly rest requirements specified in the EU drivers' hours regulations for professional drivers who are also members of the Territorial Army. The conditions of the concession are:

- a suspension of the requirement of taking a daily rest period within a period of 24 hours when the driver commenced the weekly training as a reservist or as an instructor in the cadet corps; and

- a suspension of the requirement of taking a weekly rest period at the end of the six 24 hour periods from the previous weekly rest period when the driver commences his driving as a reservist or as an instructor in the cadet corps.

A regular daily rest must still be taken before they start work for their primary employer and a regular weekly rest must be taken no later than at the end of the sixth day following training. This is due to be transposed into domestic legislation during 2011.

Chapter **17**

Users Guide to Operating Trucks and Trailers

Introduction

Presented in this chapter is a simple but comprehensive (how-to) guide to the operation of various vehicles.

Each description is split into three categories:

1. Operating Procedures: A general overview of the vehicle and how to use it.

2. Specific hazards and associated problems to be aware of.

3. Personal safety risks and physical dangers involved in carrying out the job.

Note: Many types of new vehicles have loading and un loading systems that can be operated by levers and also remote control.

P.T.O.(power take off)

In basic terms this is a large hydraulic pump which is powered by the truck engine and in turn powers all the ancillaries on the vehicle

To Engage P.T.O (Manual Transmission)

- Engine must be running

- Press clutch to the floor

- Turn the switch on

- Release the clutch-a light will then illuminate to show the P.T.O is working.

To Engage (Automatic Transmission)

- Engine must be running.

- Gear stick placed in neutral position.

- Turn the switch on.

Note: Turn switch off before driving away. **It is not advisable to drive whilst the P.T.O is engaged.**

Roll On, Roll off/ Hook Loader

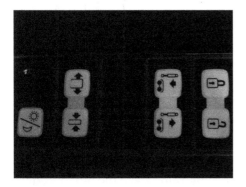
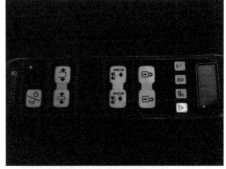

Operating procedure

Loading

- Reverse up to the bin with the hook slightly lower than the bin's catch bar.

- Check the bin doors are closed.

- Engage P.T.O.

- Use joy-stick (if modern vehicle) or control pad (if old vehicle) to operate the hook and to load bin onto vehicle.

- When it's fully on board use the button marked 'lock' to lock it into in place.

- Reverse the procedure to unload bin.

Tipping Out the Bin

- Open back doors and secure them.

- Use the joy-stick to lift the vehicle tipping ram (leave the bin locked in place).

Note: Some new trucks have retractable rear bumpers – remember to retract it before loading and unloading.

Hazards

- Overhead wires.

- Bowed back doors-these can allow the load (glass, timber) to shake out whilst driving.

- Weight of bins will be variable. Beware of overloading.

- The height of bins also varies. With a large bin you may struggle to get under a 4.5 metres / 14ft 6 bridges.

Personal Safety Risks

- Being hit by part of the load when opening doors.

- Wind can catch the doors and cause them to swing.

- Truck roll over.

Skip Truck

Operating Procedures

When loading and unloading

- Engage P.T.O.
- Lower stabilisers
- Attach 4 chains
- Sheet/un sheet the load

When Tipping

- Engage P.T.O.
- Attach 4 chains
- Lower stabilisers
- Lift up rear restraining bar
- Slide skip back against restraining bar
- Tilt skip upwards to empty

Hazards

Always secure chains together when travelling without a skip on board. This is because chains are long and heavy and will swing out at the height of a pedestrian's head or a bus window!

Personal Safety Risks

- Falling debris whilst hoisting the skip.
- Falling debris whilst un sheeting the skip
- Being struck by another truck or machine when in a noisy, busy yard.

Tipper

Operating Procedures

- Find level ground prior to tipping

- Remove load sheet and open tail board

- Engage P.T.O. Pull lever back to raise body and forward to lower.

Diff Lock

To be used in the event of the truck becoming stuck in mud. Engage the diff lock this enables power to all the drive wheels simultaneously. The switch is found on the dash board with an image of an axle on it.

Note: The vehicle must be stationary before engaging the diff lock and it must be disengaged before vehicle returns to road use.

Hazards

- Tipping; Overhead cables, high winds and frozen loads

- Stones becoming wedged between tyres, flying out under pressure smashing windscreens of following vehicles

- Punctures: periodically kick the inner tyres to see if they're sufficiently inflated

- Cuts and gashes in tyre walls rendering the tyre illegal (3 points on your licence per defective tyre)

- Driving off site with tipper body still in raised position

Personal Safety Risks

Truck rolling over.

Grab Truck

Operating Procedures

Prior to Loading

- Assess that the environment is safe. Check for pedestrians, overhead wires etc.

- Engage P.T.O

- Lower stabilisers (place a block underneath to support stabilisers if the ground is very soft.)

- Check the tailboard is closed

- Use the levers located behind the cab, or the remote control pad if in a new truck, to operate the grab

When Tipping

- Open tail board.

- Lift the grab off the load before tipping up.

All other details are the same as a Tipper.

Container Truck

Operating Procedures

Loading/once the crane has finished its lift.

- Undo chains

- Secure twist locks (locking container to trailer bed)

- Check container is thoroughly secure (check container security seal in place)

Hazards

- Doors opening whilst in transit.

- Top heavy loads

- Jammed twist locks (use a bar or hammer to free up)

Unloading

- Make sure twist locks are fully undone (if not crane will lift container, truck and trailer up into the air)

Personal Safety Risks

- Vehicle rolls over.

- Opening container doors in high wind.

Truck Mounted Crane

Full training necessary and given before use.

Operating Procedures

- Assess environment.

- Find level ground

- Engage P.T.O

- Drop load bearing stabiliser plates.

- Lower stabilisers.

- Adjust to level up the truck.

- Complete all crane checks plus chains, shackles and straps for defects and ensure they are regulation fit for intended purpose.

Hazards

- Overhead wires

- Overloading crane

- Stabilisers sinking into soft ground

- Chains or straps breaking.

- High winds

Personal Safety Risks

- Truck rollover

- Mechanical failure

- Standing underneath a suspended load.

Low Loader

Full training necessary and given before use

Step frame.

Goose neck.

Operating procedure on a goose neck trailer

- Simplified description. There are two main types of trailer, goose neck and step frame.

- The goose neck features a donkey engine, a series of moveable pins and levers. The neck detaches fully from the rest of the trailer.

- Loading takes place from either the front or over the side of the trailer.

- Other features include outriggers to extend the width of the bed.

Operating procedure on a step frame

- Undo securing chains of the ramps.

- Lower and raise ramps by using twist knobs and levers located at the rear corner of the trailer.

Hazards

- Extreme height, length or width of load (check dimensions yourself-don't trust paperwork to be correct)

- Chains, tighteners or straps working loose in transit

- Tyre blow outs (due to heat build up)

- Chains and straps breaking

Personal Safety Risks

- Chains, tighteners and straps breaking whilst being tensioned.

- Load slipping off the trailer during loading and unloading – especially in icy conditions.

- Machinery with hydraulic components **creeping down causing crush risk**

Double Deck

Full training necessary and given before use.

Operating Procedure

There are two main types of double deck trailer. The 1st Box type incorporates a fully adjustable internal floor. This can be raised and lowered using a control pad located inside the rear corner of the trailer.

The 2nd taut liner type has fixed floors and is loaded and unloaded by forklift truck.

Hazards

- Loaded incorrectly
- Top heavy
- High winds

- Low bridges (Note-due to bridge heights, companies usually assign a specific route for drivers to follow)

- On deviation from any set route, a good map is an absolute necessity – also calling the transport office may be required

Personal Safety Risks

- Vehicle roll over

- Part of load falling down on opening rear doors/curtains.

- Opening doors in windy conditions

Car Transporters

Full training necessary and given before use.

Operating Procedures

- Unloading, extend skids (ramps)
- Check car handbrake is on.
- Undo car wheel straps
- Take out wheel chocks (wedges)
- Use operating levers to adjust decks
- Reverse procedure for unloading

Note: In the event of a full load raise suspension before extending skids.

Hazards

- Low bridges/trees.
- High winds.

Personal Safety Risks

- Hijacking

Wagon and Drag (Draw Bar)

Full training given

Operating procedures

- Coupling. Basically the same as an artic apart from the use of a drop through locking pin.

  (Always make sure the pin is in and trailer brake is on before attaching air lines!)

- Hazards
- High winds

- Tight yards

- Reversing

- Personal safety risks

  Top heavy load, vehicle roll over

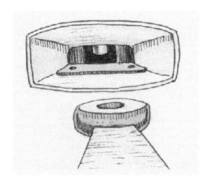

Chapter 18

ADR – Accord Dangereux Routier

(European agreement concerning the international carriage of dangerous goods by road, relating to e.g. petrol tankers, chemical tankers and explosive transporters.)

Introduction

This chapter refers to hazardous loads. It contains a short explanation of the qualifications needed, course durations and costs. The courses are individually tailored to each category of dangerous goods. All details are to be found online. These details are far too extensive and ever-changing to go into in depth here.

Courses vary from 3–7 days and they cover transporting the following.

- Explosives.

- Gasses.

- Flammable liquids.

- Flammable solids.

- Oxidising substances.

- Organic peroxides.

- Toxic & infectious substances.

- Radioactives.

- Corrosive substances.

- Miscellaneous substances.

Costs vary between £350 & £700.

Chapter 19
Mineral Products Qualification Council – MPQC

Introduction

For a driver to go to work hauling aggregates, earth or liquids, he or she must first gain a MPQC qualification. It is a very simple and straightforward course.

It covers: quarry work, tippers, truck mixers and tankers.

Drivers require an MPQC Driver Skills Card to undertake this kind of work. The aim of the course is an increased awareness of health & safety and environmental issues.

This is a 1-day course, which includes:

- Personal protective equipment (PPE).

- Preventing workplace accidents.

- Reporting incidents.

- Vehicle pre-start checks.

- Safe driving behaviour.

- Vehicle access and egress.

- Site hazards.

- Entering and leaving customer sites.

- Environmental issues.

- Vehicle-specific hazards.

Costs for this course vary between £150 and £250, and it may count as 7 hours (1 day) towards CPC course.

Chapter **20**
Umbrella Companies

Introduction

If you are new to umbrella companies, you are probably wondering:

- What is an umbrella company?

- How does it work?

- What should I do?

An umbrella company is a company which takes the role of an employer for a worker contracted through an agency.

The majority of agencies, and some companies, will only employ a driver if they are registered with one of these organisations.

- You join an umbrella company by registering online or over the phone.

- You sign an employment contract between yourself and the umbrella company.

When you join an umbrella company, study the information that they send you, as procedures differ slightly from company to company. However, they all basically work in the following way:

- At the end of the week you submit your hours and expenses to the umbrella company using their online facility.

- The umbrella company invoices the agency/company you are working for.

- The umbrella company pays you through a PAYE (pay as you earn) system after the deduction of allowable business expenses.

- At the end of the tax year, you will receive a P60 (government statement issued to taxpayers at the end of a tax year).

- Also, if relevant, you will receive a P11D (expenses and benefits form) for any beneficial expenses claimed.

The umbrella company will take an administration fee directly from your wages before paying them into your bank. Always establish what their fee is as this can vary. Try to sign up to a well-established company if possible. The company or agency you are interested in working with should recommend one to you.

Ensure that you keep a record of dates, hours and companies that you've driven for, in order to ensure that you are receiving the correct salary. Always get your time sheet signed at the end of each shift. These sheets are supplied by either the company or the agency.

It is also a good idea to keep your tachograph printouts, as, if there is any dispute with regards to pay, this provides evidence of the hours you've worked etc.

Chapter 21
Pre-Employment Examination Questions

Introduction

This chapter is comprehensive and covers most, if not all, of the questions and answers that a driver will need to know in order to pass an agency or company pre-job exam. If you study the information corresponding to these answers, you can't go wrong.

The first section covers questions and answers. The second section covers the analogue tachograph. The third section covers the Highway Code. Each subject is relevant and likely to be included, in part or in full, in a pre-job exam.

Note: it is advisable to study these pages every time you're about to change agency or company. You will need to answer 75–85% of these questions correctly in order to pass.

PRE-EMPLOYMENT QUESTIONS AND ANSWERS

Q1: A driver is required to take a statutory break after an accumulated period of driving not exceeding?

A)   3.5 hours   B)   5 hours

C)   4.5 hours   D)   4 hours

Q2: The requirement of a normal weekly rest period is?

A)   47 hours   B)   45 hours

C)   44 hours   D)   40 hours

Q3: A fortnightly driving period must not exceed?

A)   107 hours   B)   100 hours

C)   94 hours   D)   90 hours

Q4: The maximum number of hours that can be worked in a single week starting 00.00hrs on Monday is?

A)   44 hours   B)   50 hours

C)   56 hours   D)   60 hours

Q5: If splitting a 45-minute break over two periods, rules dictate the first break taken must be?

A)   30 minutes   B)   10 minutes

C)   15 minutes   D)   20 minutes

Q6: What is a period of availability?

A) Waiting time known in advance

B) Extra vehicle loading time

C) Waiting time not known in advance

D) Extra vehicle unloading time

Q7: What is classed as night-time for a heavy goods vehicle driver?

A) 01.00 – 04.00   B) 02.00 – 06.00

C) 00.00 – 04.00   D) 23.00 – 03.00

Q8: Under work time directive rules, after how many hours worked must a driver take a break?

A) 4 hours   B) 5 hours

C) 4.5 hours   D) 6 hours

Q9: If working between 6 and 9 hours, what should be the minimum break duration?

A) 60 minutes   B) 45 minutes

C) 30 minutes   D) 50 minutes

Q10: What is the maximum day shift duration for a heavy goods vehicle driver?

A) 10 hours   B) 15 hours

C) 12 hours   D) 14 hours

Q11: Generally, EU drivers' hours rules dictate that the average number of hours' driving in a day is?

A)   10 hours

B)   11 hours

C)   9 hours

D)   12 hours

Q12: Drivers can do up to how many extended driving shifts in a six-day period?

A)   1

B)   3

C)   2

D)   4

Q13: Weekly rest can be reduced to a minimum of?

A)   25 hours

B)   16 hours

C)   24 hours

D)   34 hours

14: Under normal circumstances, a driver is allowed to extend driving time twice a week to?

A)   11 hours

B)   9.5 hours

C)   10 hours

D)   12 hours

Q15: A reduction of weekly rest must be compensated for by when?

A)   End of 3rd week following the week of reduction

B)   End of 1st week following the week of reduction

C)   End of 2nd week following the week of reduction

D)   End of 4th week following the week of reduction

Q16: Pick two answers below to this question: Who is responsible for a vehicle found to be overloaded?

A)   The company

B)   The loader

C)   The driver

D)   The shunter

Q17: How long is a driver's digicard valid for?

A)   4 years

B)   10 years

C)   5 years

D)   15 years

Q18: How long do you have to report a lost or stolen digicard?

A)   10 days

B)   7 days

C)   15 days

D)   14 days

Q19: How many days of information, on average, does a driver's digicard hold?

A)   28 days

B)   60 days

C)   30 days

D)   90 days

Q20: When inserting a driver's digicard into a VU, which position and direction should the chip and arrow be in?

A)   Chip facing up and arrow pointing backwards

B)   Chip facing up and arrow pointing forwards

C)   Chip facing down and arrow pointing backwards

D)   Chip facing down and arrow pointing forwards

Q21: If you are driving a vehicle with a tachograph fitted, you must download the information on the digicard within?

A)   24 days   B)   7 days

C)   28 days   D)   14 days

Q22: If the tachograph unit breaks during a shift, what should the driver do?

A)   Call the depot   B)   Park up

C)   Keep a written record   D)   Try to fix it

Q23: Name 4 checks a driver should do on a vehicle.

A)   B)

C)   D)

Note: refer to chapter 5, vehicle checks.

Q24: What is the usual height of an unmarked bridge?

A)   15ft/4.5m   B)   16ft 6in/5.0m

C)   15ft 6in/4.7m   D)   16ft/4.8m

Q25: What is the legal speed limit for a heavy goods vehicle on:

- A-roads?

A)   40mph   B)   45mph

C)   50mph   D)   55mph

- Dual carriageways?

A) 40mph   B) 55mph

C) 50mph   D) 60mph

- Motorways?

A) 60mph   B) 65mph

C) 56mph   D) 55mph

Q26: What is the speed limiter on a heavy goods vehicle set to?

A) 50mph   B) 56mph

C) 55mph   D) 60mph

Q27: Do periods of availability (POAs) count towards a mobile worker's working time?

A) Yes   B) No

Q28: Do breaks count towards a mobile worker's working time?

A) Yes   B) No

Q29: Which two of the following factors are the most effective in making a vehicle more fuel-efficient?

A) The driver   B) Tyres

C) Lubricants   D) Aerodynamics

Q30: What is PPE?

A)   Protective personal equipment

B)   Personal protective equipment

C)   Professional protective equipment

Q31: In any 24-hour period, what is the standard minimum required rest period?

A)   9 hours   B)   10 hours

C)   11 hours   D)   12 hours

Q32: The daily rest period can be reduced 3 times a week; what is the minimum reduced daily rest period allowed?

A)   7 hours   B)   8 hours

C)   9 hours   D)   10 hours

Q33: What is the maximum number of hours that a person can work in 1 week, according to the EU work time directive?

A)   55 hours   B)   65 hours

C)   60 hours   D)   70 hours

Example of analogue tachograph chart

Tachograph Disc

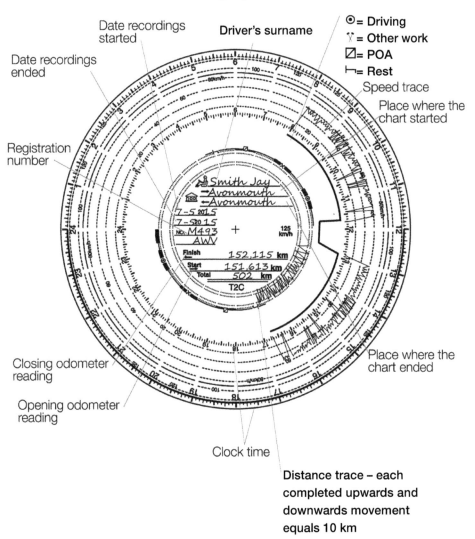

- Date recordings started
- Driver's surname
- ⊙ = Driving
- ⓨ = Other work
- ⊠ = POA
- ⊢ = Rest
- Date recordings ended
- Speed trace
- Place where the chart started
- Registration number
- Closing odometer reading
- Opening odometer reading
- Place where the chart ended
- Clock time

Distance trace – each completed upwards and downwards movement equals 10 km

Smith Jay
→Avonmouth
→Avonmouth
7 - 5 2015
7 - 5 20 15
NO. M493   +   125 km/h
AWV
Finish   152,115 km
Start   151,613 km
Total   502 km
T2C

Road markings

Mon - Sat
8 am - 6.30 pm

Loading
only

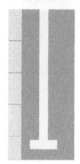

No waiting during
times shown

Loading bay

No waiting at
any time

No loading
Mon - Sat
8 am - 6.30 pm

No loading
at any time

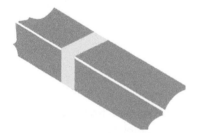

No loading or unloading
at the time shown

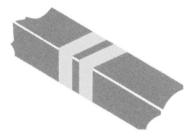

No loading or unloading
at any time

Steep hill upwards

Steep hill downwards

Fallen or falling rocks

Hump bridge

Side winds

Uneven ground

Risk of grounding

Opening or swing bridge ahead

No vehicle over width shown

No vehicle over height shown

No vehicle or combination of vehicles over length shown

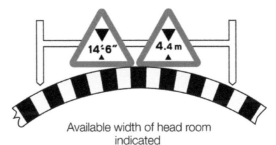
Available width of head room indicated

Weak bridge

Humps for ½ Miles

Distance over which series of road humps extends

Except for loading

No goods vehicles over maximum gross weight shown (in tonnes) except for loading

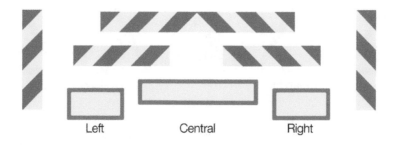

Left   Central   Right

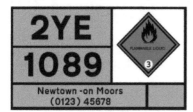

The panel illustrated is for flammable liquids.

The above panel will be displayed by vehicles carrying certain dangerous goods in packages

Oxidizing substance

Non-flammable compressed gas

Side marker

End marker

Chapter 22
Jobs at a Glance

Introduction

Below is a list of commonly found jobs, including brief descriptions, hours involved etc. This should give a window into what's out there. Everybody's different. One person might enjoy long distance and the open road. Another might enjoy multi-drop, which is more challenging and includes more physical exercise. Still another might prefer the steady, less pressurised environment provided by supermarkets, the Post Office etc.

This chapter is designed to show the types of work that are out there. It includes a brief look at what each type of job is like, so as to help with the decision of which to go for. It is always more fulfilling to have the type of job which best suits you.

Skips

Short hours, usually 7am–5pm weekdays and 7am–1pm Saturdays. This is usually local work. You should expect this type of work to be very dirty. It's a busy job; drivers are expected to get on and do as many skips as possible on top of collecting cash from customers. It will risk your licence if anything drops off onto the road, so be careful not to rush.

Tippers

On muck shifting and aggregate deliveries, it's usually 7am–5pm weekdays and 7am–1pm Saturdays. This job is all about getting as many loads in as possible in a day. Again, you should expect this to be fairly dirty work. It may risk your licence if you are over-weight on earth-shifting work. Quarry work is OK because truck is weighed.

Multi-drop

Reasonably high-pressured job; it can be time-sensitive regarding deliveries. There's also the risk of personal injury due to hurrying whilst loading and unloading. The job becomes easier if you are allocated a regular route and get to know where the drops are. A good knowledge of the local area always helps. Average 10–15 hour shifts.

Brewery deliveries

Usually 7am–5pm. This is local work, similar to multi-drop, but with less pressure. You will get plenty of exercise on the job. Plus the chance of getting a regular route is reasonably high.

General haulage

General haulage could involve transporting anything from palletised goods to car parts. The companies in this field are very competitive. Employers usually expect you to work lots of hours, so there is no guarantee of getting home every night, especially if you are doing long distance. Start and finish times vary. Can be unsociable hours and fairly flat-out work; however, it is relatively easy to get work in this area. It might be a good way to earn some much needed experience, though it may very well be a baptism by fire. Expect 10–15 hour shifts.

Supermarkets

Class 1 – usually 2 drops a day or 2 trailer swaps. Rarely more than 6. Class 2 – between 2 and 5 drops. Employers usually expect you to have a couple of years' experience. Expect good equipment and working conditions – goods are usually palletised and caged, making the process quite simple. You will not be pressured to speed out on the road, but expect employers to be quite pedantic about paperwork and driver behaviour. Varying start times, 10 hours is an average shift.

Shipping containers

This is mainly long distance work. Many companies do not expect the driver to load and unload due to insurance. Various start times. Average 10–12 hour shifts.

Car transporters

Experience in this line of work is crucial. Good pay due to added pressure because of high insurance costs to companies regarding damage to cars etc. Obvious considerations for driver include hazards such as low-hanging branches, theft etc. You will be expected to load and unload – drive cars up and down the ramps without damaging them. Various start times. Average 10–12 hour shifts.

ADR

Good pay, driver required to do lots of training. There are extensive rules and regulations. Can be dangerous, involves hauling potentially explosive loads. Various start times. Average 10–12 hour shifts.

Music theatre and film work

Much of this is seasonal work, but it is well paid and interesting. Nice people. Hours vary wildly. Potentially a lot of down time on location.

Chapter 23

Jobs Abroad

Introduction

This chapter is a brief look at the job opportunities abroad. There are many countries which a UK driver could consider going to work in. I have chosen to focus on the examples given due to the probability of work and the standard of living.

Job Opportunities Abroad

The country most interested in hiring UK LGV1 drivers is Canada. You have to go through an agency; they do all the necessary paperwork, e.g. temporary visa, plus arrange a job. It costs around £3,000 in stage payments. You need to take a short LGV test for left-hand drive trucks in Canada. The government criterion is to fill long haul vacancies. If all goes well, it equates to only 3 years' long distance interstate driving before you are entitled to full residency. On average, 3 weeks out of 4 will be spent living in the truck. You can apply for full residency after working for 18 months. This may take a further 12 to 18 months

to be processed. Once residency is granted, you can change to whatever job suits you. You will need to be very careful and check out the agency before using them. Some have been known to be bogus scam artists.

If you are considering emigrating to Canada, a humorous and informative web resource is Trucker Josh VLOGS on YouTube: www.youtube.com/user/truckerjosh456.

Australia and New Zealand are also possibilities, but are much harder to get into. And you will need to work for 5 years before any company can sponsor you for residency; this still may or may not be granted. It's a gamble, but sometimes nothing ventured, nothing gained. On a plus point, being right-hand drive, there is no LGV test to take. UK licences are valid.

Good luck if you decide to emigrate!

Chapter 24
Optional Electrical Equipment

Introduction

This chapter outlines some of the very helpful, optional electrical equipment that is available. I have chosen to focus on two types of equipment: sat navs and the Pure Highway DAB radio adaptor. One will ensure that you don't get lost and lose time on deliveries, the other will ensure that you don't die of boredom on the way there.

As far as my experience with sat navs goes, this information is very accurate.

Sat navs

Sat navs are an absolutely tremendous bit of kit. They take a serious amount of pressure out of the job. When you key in the dimensions and weight etc. the sat nav will help to guide you away from any potential hazards such as low bridges, weak bridges and weight restricted roads.

The **best** sat navs by far are the big name brands. The most expensive models cost around £350 to £400. I found others priced at £50 to £300 pretty much useless.

Note: I recommend fitting it lower down on the windscreen and putting a small pillow or something similarly soft underneath it. I have had the unit come loose and drop off a few times: a very valuable piece of equipment to break!

Pure Highway DAB radio adaptor

When out on the road, good entertainment is good company. If your truck doesn't have a digital radio, it is possible to transfer a DAB signal into your truck radio through a Pure Highway device.

This device plugs into the cigarette lighter/electrical power-point. It has its own aerial. Simply set the frequency on the device, then set the radio to the same frequency. It enables access to all DAB channels, including 6 Music (real quality entertainment!). It costs around £70. The signal is very good in most places, but it can be lost in rural areas. It's a great bit of kit!

Note: the aerial it's supplied with is not designed to be installed numerous times. In order to avoid numerous aerial purchases, you should consider buying a magmount aerial which is compatible with a Pure Highway. A magmount aerial has a thicker cable and, as it is magnetic, will easily stick to anything metal in the cab. It should cost around £10 and can be found online.

Chapter 25
Road Safety/Useful Information

Introduction

This chapter contains useful tips and advice for various situations which drivers may find themselves in. My main piece of advice is – never forget how much time and money went into gaining your LGV or PCV licence and how easy it is to lose it. If you are unsure of something, ask for help. If you ever find yourself being pressured into doing something illegal, just walk away. There's always another day, another job. The laws are so strong now; it's just not worth the risk!

Road Safety

Temporary road works
Be aware that some temporary road works sites do not have signs placed far enough back to give you enough, or even any warning. During busy times, such as rush hour, cars etc may be queuing way back beyond sight of the signs. Therefore, always insure that you slow down when approaching a

blind bend, because a fully laden truck will not be able to stop at a moments notice. This is not an uncommon situation; you will come across it in the course of your career.

Tyre scrub build up/Spring summer
During the hotter period of the year scrub builds up on the road surface. In itself not a real problem until the first heavy rain shower which turns it back into oil. Be ready for this hazard, the road can very suddenly turn into a skating ring. Heavy trucks slide easily..

Autumn
Same scenario, but add a covering of wet leaves and the road becomes even slippyer. Hit the brakes and truck just slides.

Turning off the motorway
If, when you are planning to turn onto a slip road, your vision is obscured whilst following another truck or coach, ensure you slow down in order to create space to see. There could potentially be a queue of traffic extending to the edge of the carriageway that you are not aware of.

Wasps, bees and spiders
These can be an instantaneous hazard. There are numerous accidents every year due to driver's attention being diverted away from the road for a second or two.

I've personally heard of at least one fatality. A passing car driver saw an oncoming truck driver doing battle with a bee. The truck veered off the road and hit a farm wall head on.

Slamming into reverse
Avoid stopping quickly and then instantly beginning to reverse. Give time for a possible cyclist or motorcyclist to take evasive action (they do not have a reverse gear and you will not hear them). I have seen a motorcyclist backpedalling a heavy bike for all he was worth trying to get out the way of a quickly reversing truck.

Blind spots/cyclists listening to music
Cyclists and motorcyclists have a nasty habit of creeping up the nearside of trucks undetected or stopping directly in front, below windscreen level at a

set of traffic lights/junction. Be mindful of them getting part of their clothing or bag caught up on the side of the truck and being dragged underneath. In the past there have been several very serious incidents of cyclists/motorcyclists sitting in the blind spots of truck mirrors. In a rush the truck driver suddenly changed his/her mind about which route to take. Without indicating they turned suddenly, thus leaving no time for the person to react (you can guess the rest).

Black ice

This Is an unseen danger, especially found on untreated roads and shady areas after the temperature drops below freezing. I spoke to an artic driver who hit a stretch of black ice whilst driving at speed in the middle lane of a motorway. The trailer started sliding sidewards pulling the tractor unit out of line (pre-jack knife) He managed to gently ease off the accelerator and slowly, as the speed decreased, it all came back under control and into line. He was fortunate

Blinding low winter sun

A real hazard, especially when travelling towards the sun whilst cresting a hill. I know of a driver who crested a hill and was sun blinded and completely unable to see anything for a few seconds. At the last moment, still partially blinded, he saw a queue of traffic. He swerved to the left to avoid it and by doing so accidentally hit a lady walking her dog. The driver, subsequently traumatised, then faced manslaughter charges for over two years until the case was finally dropped.

Where safe to do so, if you can't see- slow down. Drive defensively to anticipate the sun's level.

Different truck/trailer height

Identical looking truck and trailers can be deceivingly lower or higher than you might expect. Always look for the height written on them

Note: a brand-new truck or trailer can have a shiny, slippery floor making for a much higher possibility of load moving in transit. Load needs to be secured tightly to prevent risk of truck rollover on tight bends.

Mobile phone

This is obviously a major distraction to concentration and a big risk to license. A much bigger problem occurs in the event of an accident involving a fatality. The driver can then be charged with manslaughter. I have heard tell of a driver being involved in an accident. The police seized his phone and inserted a code. By doing this they were able to see all phone use prior to the accident.

Horses

Horses are very easily spooked when they come into close proximity with a moving truck-ideally pull over to the side of the road, switch off your engine then let them pass. If it's a tight space then very slowly crawl past them whilst looking for any possible signals from the rider to advance, or stop and switch off.

Useful Information

Included here is a short list of work-wear and useful gear.

Work-wear:

- Steel toecap boots

- High-visibility jacket or vest

- Gloves

- Waterproofs

Useful gear:

- Map

- Notepad and pens

- Torch

- Screwdrivers

- Mole grips

- Adjustable spanner

- Bungee straps

- Duct tape

- Ice scraper

- Disinfectant wet wipes

- Plasters and bandages

Tips and advice

1. Keep diary of dates, hours worked, rest, POA and of any problems etc. Also, ensure you keep the tacho printouts.

2. Away from yard, photocopy company driver sheet etc. (can be difficult to use). This gives you time to study and get used to it on your own terms.

3. Set the height to current trailer to avoid bridge strikes. If you

are stopped by DVSA and it is incorrect, there is a high probability of a fine.

4. During blindsided reversing, if the trailer becomes impossible to see because of the articulation angle, pull out the passenger mirror a click or two.

5. Try, if possible, not to rely too heavily on the person giving

guidance in a manoeuvre through a tight space. If safe, keep getting out to check yourself. If there is an accident, 9 times out of 10 the driver will get the blame.

6. Adjusting the lift axle into the up position can be useful in wet conditions whilst tug testing after coupling to trailer (puts more weight onto drive axle). This also aids traction on slippery ramps, inclines and during tight manoeuvres.

7. Brake fade can occur when driving down long steep hills carrying heavy loads. Ideally, slow vehicle with gears and apply footbrake intermittently, not continuously. (If brakes overheat, the drums expand away from the shoes causing less effective braking.)

8. Check wheel nuts by eye and by hand, try at least 3 on each wheel.

9. Hijackers usually target expensive loads such as cigarettes and alcohol, but not always. Anything that can be sold on a market stall is fair game. It has also been known for them to target new trucks and trailers for re-sale abroad. If you are stopped by DVSA, it is apparently within a driver's rights to lock the cab doors and shout through the window or write on paper a message to state that you will not open up, but will follow a DVSA vehicle to one of their designated yards. Criminals have been known to impersonate DVSA and police officers.

An article published recently said that there is a concern over stolen DVSA security uniforms in the northwest being used in bogus stops on goods vehicles. The advice given is that all

DVSA vehicles have a roof bar matrix sign. DVSA do not use vehicles with rear window matrix signs??

10. Every transport company must have an O licence (operator's licence), which should be displayed in the windscreen of the vehicle.

11. A lot of new trucks have automatic gearboxes. Select 'drive' ('D') or automatic ('A'), depending on the box. Some gear levers are counter-intuitive i.e. push the lever forward to reverse, pull it back to go forward.

12. Coupling heights – if you are unsure if a trailer is too high to couple to, reverse halfway under until the fifth wheel is only half visible. Lift the truck suspension until you feel the weight of the trailer and then reverse under.

13. Take extreme care to ensure that the handbrake is always applied correctly during coupling and uncoupling procedures. **A runaway is definitely no fun!**

14. A good system after coupling up is to follow this sequence:

    - Fit the fifth wheel dog clip.
    - Take the trailer brake off.
    - Wind up the legs.
    - Fit the number plate, then carry out all necessary checks.

15. If the airline is difficult to fit, jiggling it can help. Alternatively, repeatedly press the foot brake in order to lower the air pressure.

16. Many a driver's undoing is being distracted by someone or something, during the coupling/uncoupling process. If this

happens, retrace all previous steps taken in the sequence **before** carrying on.

17. Top-heavy loads are dangerous. Go steadily and carefully around bends. There is a possible risk of rollover, injuries to you (the driver), and of completely crushing a car if it's alongside. (Double-decker trailers and containers are the most risky.)

18. AdBlue is a type of chemical solution designed to reduce a vehicle's nitrogen oxide emissions. All modern goods vehicles are fitted with an AdBlue tank. Roughly, 1 litre should last 100 miles.

19. All drivers must complete 35 hours of periodic training every five years on an ongoing basis to be able to drive a truck or bus. Periodic training is delivered through courses that consist in length of a total of 35 hours, split into five 7-hour days. The easiest, least intense way of doing this is a day a month for five months before the expiry date. Prices usually start at £250 and run right up to £600. Shop around for the best deal.

20. Depending on which company you work for, your vehicle may be fitted with an Isotrak system. Isotrak systems are used by some transport companies in order to track trucks, trailers and loads. An Isotrak system can also be used as a contact link between a driver and their company office. If your company does use Isotrak systems, they should provide you with full instruction and training. Although it looks complicated, it is fairly simple to use.

21. Audiobooks can be a great way of keeping yourself entertained on the road. You could potentially learn something whilst you work or just listen to interesting stories.

Noisy yards

Be aware of other trucks manoeuvring around you. Pay attention especially in busy noisy yards when stood at the side of a trailer, winding landing gear, at the front of it undoing a lock or adjusting a fridge temperature etc. There is a strong possibility of not being able to hear another truck bearing down on you!!

Over speeding

In the event of over speeding the tachograph unit will start to flash, thus bringing your awareness to this mistake. Simply press OK to clear screen, when safe to do so.

Gantry speed cameras

Pay special attention to these variable speed limit cameras. It is very easy when tired or irritated to make the following mistakes.

1. Looking at speed limit of the first camera, and then taking this to be limit for the whole stretch of road.

2. Become distracted by something, someone's bad driving etc Forget to look up at subsequent gantry signs, which by now may have altered to a lower speed.

Rear steer

Rear steering trucks and trailers obviously handle very differently to none rear steer out on the road. Drive steadily. Take time to get used to the differences

Agencies

Large companies usually have one main agency and a few smaller agencies supplying drivers. It is worth finding out who is the main agency, as they will have most of the work. Either speak to one of their drivers or go to the company directly and ask which agency they use. Large companies often specify at least two years LGV experience. Often during busy periods, summer and Christmas these rules are waived. This is a good time to try and get in. Once you are in your in.

Children and animals

Children sometimes manage to escape from parents. They will have no qualms about running straight out into the road chasing a ball or climbing under a stationary truck.

I know of a dog running under a truck on a weighbridge. The truck engine was running, the lady instinctively and immediately climbed under the truck after the dog.(Unforeseen events do happen!)

YouTube

YouTube can be a very useful resource for learning how to do everything from a tachograph manual entry to coupling up an artic.

Cab night heater

Usually located on the dash board or on the back panel inside the cab. It is self explanatory to use apart from the on switch needs to be continuously pressed for a few seconds until illuminated .

Adjusting the steering wheel position

New trucks are fitted with a button / lever located on the cowelling or on the floor. This allows the height or angle to be altered to the drivers preference.

Tyres

- Check the tread depth, and for splits in the side walls of the tyre. Tyres that are just on, or around, the legal limit of 1mm at the start of a shift can wear down and become illegal during the same day if you are travelling long distance, especially in hot weather. It's 3 points on your licence plus a fine for each defective tyre. Four illegal tyres and it could be game over! Check and double-check. Ask someone if in doubt; don't take it out!

- A trucker's atlas is always a very useful item to have in the cab. It will indicate all bridge heights and weight restrictions etc. Usually around £10 to purchase.

- If you are unsure whether you are able to manoeuvre around a tight bend in a built-up area, then, when it's safe, take up two lanes. At times this is the only way possible to get around.

Chapter 26
Driver Fatigue

Driver fatigue and falling asleep at the wheel

How to know when you are suffering from serious driver fatigue – **example scenario:**

Your eyelids become heavy and constantly try to close, your head starts to nod. You can't stop yawning and you find it hard to focus.

Suddenly you become aware of the rumble strips; you blink hard and realise that you have veered onto the hard shoulder for a moment and quickly straighten the wheel. You were asleep; this time you were lucky ...

Serious fatigue symptoms:

- Frequent blinking, difficulty focusing and droopy eyelids.

- Daydreaming/scrambled thoughts.

- Missing exits and street signs, an inability to remember last few miles driven.

- Constant yawning/sore eyes.

- Head feels heavy.

- Drifting across lanes, hitting the rumble strip of hard shoulder and tailgating.

- Suddenly being aware of getting too close to another vehicle.

- Feeling restless, irritable and confused.

Temporary cures:

- Open both windows and turn up the radio loud.

- Sugary foods and caffeine-containing drinks.

- Pinch yourself to feel slight pain, and keep pinching.

- Say something aloud or sing.

If absolutely exhausted, you will have no prior warning or control over falling asleep, it will just happen. **Pull over and stop!** Take a 20-minute sleep break, get up, take a brisk walk. If you are still exhausted, sleep for another hour or two. Sometimes you have to just give in to the situation; it is better to accept any potential repercussions for being late etc. rather than endanger yourself or an innocent person/family. **There are other people's lives in your hands, not just your own!**

Note: (motorway driving): If you need to stop immediately you can park up at the top end of the motorway slip road just after the 'motorway start/end' sign and sleep there.

Chapter 27

Load securing, operators' guide

Taken from; GOV.UK Load securing: Operators guide. Updated 16th October 2017.

Introduction

This DVSA instruction chapter is aimed at the vehicle owners and operators.

Do not be daunted by this chapter. Training is usually given on operating all vehicles apart from dry box vans and tautliners. The reasons for the inclusion of this chapter are:

- As a tool to be dipped into to reaffirm the training and advice you've received is correct.

- Give prior knowledge of what to expect before changing from one type of vehicle to another.

- As a learning aid for helping to grow your knowledge on properly securing all types of loads.

- For yours and the publics safety.

- To protect your licence and wallet by understanding the regulations the DVSA expect you to abide by.

1

1.1 Why load securing is important

DVSA is responsible for lorry, bus and coach enforcement including:

- roadworthiness – including both the vehicle and the load it's carrying

- traffic enforcement – including drivers' hours and overloading

During 2013, DVSA issued over 2,000 prohibitions to vehicles which presented a road safety risk because of how their load was secured.

22,000 road impact incidents

There were 22,000 road impact incidents in England in 2013 caused by objects falling from vehicles.

In the same period, the Highways Agency reported over 22,000 road impact incidents caused by objects falling from vehicles. This is dangerous to all road users.

This resulted in the closure of either a single lane or the full carriageway. On average, it takes 20 minutes to deal with each incident.

This places a significant financial burden on the UK economy from:

- time wasted in traffic
- damage to goods
- damage to infrastructure.

1.2 About this guidance

This guidance has been produced by DVSA and representatives from the transport industry. The subject matters chosen were the areas causing the greatest industry concern.

For the benefit of this guidance any reference to vehicle should be read as any vehicle, trailer or combination unless specified otherwise.

1.3 Load securing systems

The load securing systems you use should be appropriate for both:

- the loads being carried
- the vehicles being used

These may include:

- 'over-the-top' lashings
- rear kites
- intermediate bulk heads
- direct lashing to specific anchor points

Whoever is responsible for loading a vehicle needs to consider other important factors like axle weights and vehicle stability. These are the fundamental requirements in making sure vehicles are safe before starting a journey.

2. Load securing: the basics

In this section:

- **good practice**
- **make sure the vehicle is fit for purpose**
- **load the vehicle properly**
- **choose the most appropriate securing method**
- **use adequate load restraint**
- **communication is important**
- **load restraint system**

2.1 Good practice – see DVSA video:

https://www.gov.uk/government/publications/load-securing-vehicle-operator-guidance/load-securing-vehicle-operator-guidance

2.2 Make sure the vehicle is fit for purpose

You should consider the types of loads being carried when buying vehicles.

There are aftermarket products which can provide bespoke securing products to adapt vehicles to ensure they're fit for purpose.

There are also specialist companies who can give advice on the right load securing system for your operation and the loads you carry. The relevant trade body for your business may be able to help their members.

2.3 Load the vehicle properly

Stack the load against the headboard with the centre of gravity as low as possible. Make sure it's stable without lashings to reduce the risk of it falling over during unloading.

If the load isn't stable by itself, think about how you can support it: put it in a box, stillage or transport frame.

If the load isn't against the headboard – or items could slide over it – think about other ways you can stop the load from moving forward. You may need extra lashings, sails, chocks or blocking.

The headboard is a key part of the load securing system – fix any damage as soon as possible.

2.4 Choose the right securing method

Whatever method you choose, the load restraint system needs to secure the load to the vehicle chassis and prevent movement.

Not all loads or vehicles are the same. Choose a securing system that stops the load moving without creating other risks – like unnecessary manual handling and working at height.

Webbing straps or chains are often used to secure loads, but they aren't right for every situation. For example fragile or live loads need different securing methods to prevent damage.

2.5 Use adequate load restraint

Incidents happen when drivers and operators underestimate how much restraint is needed to keep a load on the vehicle.

Dynamic forces are much higher than static forces. For example, more force is required to secure a load when it is moving (dynamic) than when it is stationary (static).

2.6 Communication is important

Fatal and serious injuries don't usually 'just happen'. Generally, there are some minor incidents and near misses beforehand.

Reporting these and other issues – such as restricted access to delivery sites – can help prevent a more serious situation in the future.

Give drivers clear information about:

- the loads they carry

- how to unload

- what they should do if the load shifts

This is particularly important if the driver hasn't loaded their vehicle or trailer. It's useful for everyone involved if a loading plan is provided.

2.7 Load restraint system

The combined strength of the load restraint system must be sufficient to withstand a forwards force not less than the total weight of the load to prevent the load moving under severe braking, and half the weight of the load moving backwards and sideways.

Even at low speeds, the forces acting on a load when the vehicle is moving can be high enough for the load to move.

Heavy loads can and do move and the weight of the load alone should never be relied on to hold the load in place.

Once moving, forces to prevent the load from continuing to move are much higher than if the load was static.

3. Responsibility for load securing

In this section:

- **general responsibilities**

- **responsibility for loading vehicles**

- **responsibility for unloading vehicles**

- **responsibility for hauling the load**

3.1 General responsibilities

The driver isn't the only person responsible for the safety of the vehicle and its load.

Everybody in the transport chain should make themselves aware of the rules set out in the <u>DfT code of practice: safety of loads on vehicles.</u>

You may also find the the <u>European best practices guidelines on cargo securing for road transport (PDF, 24.9MB, 96 pages)</u> helpful.

Stay up to date

DVSA regularly updates its '<u>Moving On</u>' blog which gives official advice and information for lorry, bus and van operators and drivers. You can also sign up to get email alerts when new posts are published.

The trade associations also provide regular updates.

Health and safety

Employers have specific responsibilities under the Health and Safety at Work Act 1974 and The Management of Health & Safety at Work Regulations 1999 to ensure the health and safety of:

- their employees

- anyone else affected by their work activities

Risk assessment

Risk assessment is a legal requirement that helps you to identify issues and take reasonably practicable steps to control the risks.

This should help reduce the chances of problems occurring, but you should think about what happens if the load shifts in transit.

Drivers shouldn't be expected to deal with an unsafe load alone at the roadside.

Read <u>guidance about risk management</u> on the HSE website.

3.2 Responsibility for loading vehicles

If you're responsible for loading vehicles, you should make sure that they're loaded so the load remains in a safe condition during:

- loading

- transit

- unloading

You should decide:

- who will carry out the loading

- what training they should have

- how they will be supervised

Involve drivers in the loading process if possible

If the drivers don't load the vehicle ideally they should be given the opportunity to observe the competent person loading the vehicle.

If it's not appropriate for the drivers to watch the loading then they should be given information about how the load has been secured and/or given the chance to check the load prior to departure.

If a driver isn't happy with how the load is secured or how stable it is, you should make sure that the load is:

- assessed by a competent person

- reloaded or re secured if necessary

Report load shifts

Drivers should be asked to report load shifts so that you can take action to deal with it safely and stop it happening again.

Loads can move even under normal driving conditions so don't automatically assume the driver is at fault if the load shifts during a journey.

Appropriate method of load securing

You, or a competent person appointed by you, should decide on the most appropriate method of load securing for the load and the vehicle.

You should provide safe access (such as working platforms or access ladders) if the chosen method involves drivers or loaders accessing the trailer bed.

It's good practice to involve those actually doing the loading in the decision-making process, as they may be able to identify practical solutions.

Loading plan

You may find it useful to develop a loading plan for the loads you transport.

It's important to communicate with both the haulier and the delivery site when preparing the loading plan so that everyone knows what they're responsible for.

You should think about:

- how the load is to be unloaded

- what happens if the load shifts in transit

Information about the load should be clearly communicated to the driver. You need to take account of possible driver handovers and language barriers.

A loading docket that travels with the load may help to communicate information to the haulier and the delivery site. This can be as simple as a sketch showing the position of the load and the load securing system.

The driver should be made aware of what's expected of them at the delivery site, including things like whether they should:

- report to security on arrival

- stay in their cab during unloading or if they're expected to help unloading

3.3 Responsibility for unloading vehicles

Many of the same principles will apply if you're responsible for unloading vehicles.

You can help drivers and operators by providing clear information about:

- what's expected on your site

- who's responsible for what

Vehicles that arrive with a shifted load

You should think about what happens if a vehicle arrives at your site with a shifted load.

A vehicle in a potentially dangerous condition shouldn't be sent back onto the public highway. It should be moved to a quarantined area where:

- its condition can be assessed

- a decision made about how best to unload it

3.4 Responsibility for hauling the load

If you're responsible for hauling the load, you should make sure that:

- you're using a suitable vehicle for the task

- the vehicle is loaded so that it's safe for transport on the road

Communicate with suppliers, the delivery site and driver

You should communicate with both the supplier and the delivery site so that:

- any issues can be identified

- remedial action taken before they become problems

Wherever possible, drivers should be involved in the loading process. Their experience may help the loader(s) identify any problems before the vehicle sets out on its journey.

Secure the load

The load should be secured to the trailer before the driver takes it out on the road. You should:

- agree the method(s) of load restraint with the supplier

- make sure that the vehicle is suitable for the method chosen (like, for restraint bars you need to make sure that the correct type of side rail is fitted)

If loads are to be secured using webbing straps and/or chains, you need to make sure that they can be secured either:

- directly to the chassis of the trailer

- to rated attachment points

Rope hooks aren't suitable attachment points. Straps and chains shouldn't be used in the same assembly.

4. Consequences of poor load securing

In this section:

- **death or serious injury**

- **damaged reputation**

- **prosecution**

4.1 Death or serious injury

First and foremost, it can result in death or serious injury.

It can have serious consequences for the driver, other road users, and anyone involved with unloading the vehicle.

HSE statistics show that workplace transport is one of the highest risk work activities, accounting for over half of all death or injury incidents reported to HSE.

Many incidents are a direct result of poor load securing, for example:

- items falling out of any vehicle when the curtain is opened for unloading and hitting someone stood next to the vehicle

- items falling out of a vehicle during unloading, causing someone to jump out of the way and fall

- poorly-secured loads collapsing or falling over during the journey so they have to be unloaded by hand, and someone then slipping over on the load bed or falling from the vehicle

- damage to goods, property or the infrastructure, which will eventually be passed onto the consumer

- damaged roads, which may themselves lead to more wear and tear on vehicles resulting in increased overheads for the operator

Your corporate reputation may well suffer if you're involved in a load securing incident. This could be as a result of:

- adverse publicity in the press

- loss of contracts due to damaged goods etc

4.3 Prosecution

You could be prosecuted for causing the death of an employee or a member of the public due to negligence on their part.

Negligence could be viewed as ignorance or the lack of effective processes, like failing to comply with existing guidance. This can result in substantial fines for the company or individuals in the case of a partnership or sole trader.

5. Enforcement

In this section:

- **how DVSA assesses how loads are secured**

- **load security matrix**

- **prohibition and fixed penalty**

- **penalty points**

- **other action**

5.1 How DVSA assesses how loads are secured

DVSA deals with load securing under the following laws:

- The Road Vehicles (Construction and Use) Regulations 1986, regulation 100

- The Road Traffic Act 1988, section 40a

DVSA examiners ask themselves a series of questions:

- can the load slide or topple forwards or backwards?

- can the load slide or topple off the side?

- is the load unstable?

- is the load securing equipment in poor condition?

- is there anything loose that might fall off?

- does the vehicle present an immediate likelihood of causing danger of injury due to its load security or stability?

The examiner will refer to the load security matrix if they answer 'yes' to any of these questions. The matrix helps them decide the appropriate course of action to take based on the risk.

Encourage drivers to ask these questions

You can encourage your drivers to ask the same questions before the start of any journey. This will:

- help identify potential problems

- make sure load securing remains high on the drivers' agenda

5.2 Load security matrix

The load security matrix has 3 tables showing:

- the risk represented by the type of load

- the type of load securing used

- what action to take based on where a load and its security fit within the previous tables

Risk represented by the type of load

This table shows examples of the different load types, but there are other kinds.

Load type A	Load type B	Load type C
Metal pipes, sheet or bar	Timber	Clothing
Reinforced concrete	FIBCs/bulk powder	Wood chip
Bricks, stone or concrete	Roll cages	Waste paper
Vehicles including scrap	Bagged aggregate	Coal bags
Plant machinery	Empty skips stacked 3 high	Bulk material (in tipper)
Reels including steel, wire or paper	Heavy palletised goods	Packaging material
Kegs and barrels		Single loaded skips
Stacked loaded skips		Empty skips less than 3 high
Empty skips stacked more than 3 high		Light palletised goods
Metal casings		
Glass		
Containers or work cabins		

Type of load security used

Defect category 1	Defect category 2	Defect category 3
No load securing	>30cm gap between load and vehicle headboard	Lashings on ropehooks
> 1m gap between front of load and vehicle headboard	Unsheeted load in bulk tipper or skip	Minor damage to headboard not affecting structural integrity

Appropriate action

Load type	Defect category 1	Defect category 2	Defect category 3
Load type A	Prohibit	Prohibit	Advise
Load type B	Prohibit	Prohibit/Advise	Advise
Load type C	Prohibit	Advise	Advise

You can't consider the vehicle's headboard part of the load securing system if there are large gaps between it and the load. If there are, then you need to find other ways of preventing forward movement.

5.3 Prohibition and fixed penalty

A prohibition prevents the vehicle from being moved until the load securing problem is fixed.

When a prohibition is issued, the driver is given a fixed penalty notice.

The driver then has 60 minutes to fix the problem. If they can't do this, then the DVSA immobilisation policy would be followed with a release fee incurred.

5.4 Penalty points

Penalty points aren't routinely issued, but they can be in certain situations, for example where a vehicle is deemed to be in a dangerous condition due to the condition or suitable purpose, or weight, distribution, packing and adjustment of the load.

> **This offence carries 3 penalty points and a licence endorsement for the driver. The court may also give the driver an unlimited fine.**

All vehicles with load securing issues are dangerous, but some are a more significant risk than others.

For example, no load securing on a flat-bed vehicle carrying a load of steel would be considered substantially more dangerous than a curtain-side vehicle laden with a few loose bags of clothing.

The vehicle carrying steel could result in a charge of dangerous condition, whereas a less serious offence might result in the driver being given advice or a verbal warning.

5.5 Other action

Depending on how serious the load securing breach is, DVSA can interview you about the issues found at the roadside. This action could result in either:

- legal proceedings against you

- a report to the Traffic Commissioner (TC)

Following consideration of any DVSA report, the TC may take regulatory action for failure to comply with the undertaking of an operator's licence. Disciplinary action could include suspension, curtailment or revocation of your licence.

The TC also has the power to take action against a driver's vocational licence, such as a suspension. Not only will this have an adverse impact on the driver, it might also create additional problems for the operator.

Prohibitions also adversely impact on an operator's compliance risk score (OCRS).

6. Types of vehicles

In this section:

- **curtain-sided bodies and EN 12642 XL rating**

- **double-deck trailers**

- **rigid-sided vehicles**

- **euroliner vehicles and trailers**

6.1 Curtain-sided bodies and EN 12642 XL rating

Even with load retaining curtains, a standard curtain-sided vehicle or trailer body won't normally give enough load securing.

The body structure and curtains only provide weather protection for the load. Load and secure goods the same as you would on a flatbed vehicle.

EN 12642 (BS EN 12642 in the UK) is a build standard for vehicle and trailer bodies. It sets out two types that can be built:

- standard body types (L)

- reinforced body types (XL)

Vehicle and trailer bodies don't have to be built to this standard in the UK but **XL bodies** are a useful part of the load securing system.

Light goods
You can secure goods or unstacked pallets that weigh less than 400kg per item:

- using buckle straps that hang from the roof of the body structure

- with inner curtains – *see light palletised goods*

Treat goods and pallets over 400kg – and stacked pallets if the combined weight of the stack is more than 400kg– as heavy goods.

Heavy goods

Secure heavy goods that weigh more than 400kg per item or pallet with:

- lashing

- load-rated nets

- tarpaulins with integral straps

Whatever method you use, it must be able to restrain half the weight of the load to the side and rear, and the full weight forward.

This is the minimum standard for normal road driving.

In most cases, the load carried and the body structure used will show the best way to secure the load.

Both the DfT and EU guides provide detailed instructions on how to secure different loads depending on things like:

- materials

- weight

- friction between the load and the load bed

Tests on ordinary trailers show that the weakest point is the frame.

This highlights the limited benefits of attaching stronger curtains to ordinary trailers.

EN 12642 XL

XL rated bodies display stickers in prominent positions.

Trailers and vehicles built to the EN 12642 XL standard can withstand a minimum of 40% of the rated payload to the side – without extra load securing – when following the manufacturer's guidance.

DVSA accept an EN 12642 XL rated vehicle/trailer keeping 50% of the rated payload to the side without any extra securing, as long as the load fills the entire load area to the front, rear and to within 80mm of the side. This is often called a 'positive fit'.

It's acceptable to fit lateral bulkheads or use packing material to fill any gaps in the load to guarantee positive fit when loading.

Using XL rated vehicles to transport diminishing or part loads isn't ideal but it's still possible as long as the following are met:-

- any gaps created by a diminishing load are blocked keeping a positive fit

- a partial load which doesn't fill the load area has extra securing – this should be enough to meet the DfT rules: 50% to the side, rear and 100% to the front

For example, the use of rated lashing straps across the rear of the load must provide security for 50% of the entire load. This will secure the load in the same way as the rear of the vehicle would for a full load.

Or, the load should be secured as it would in a non-'XL' rated vehicle.

The EN 12642 XL standard refers to the entire vehicle or trailer and not just the curtains. So, reinforced curtains fitted to an ordinary trailer don't meet the XL standard. There's no such thing as an 'XL curtain'.

XL-rated bodies have stickers in prominent positions – usually on the rear door or front bulkhead – to show they meet the standard.

The curtains of an XL-rated body also have to be built to EN 12641.

Stickers confirming this are usually found on the inside of the curtains at the rear of the body.

XL stickers should provide the following information:

- confirmation that the body structure – not just the curtain sides – meets the EN 12642 XL standard

- the name of the vehicle or trailer manufacturer

- the year of manufacture

XL bodies are also given a certificate, specific to the vehicle tested, from the organisation responsible for testing vehicles and trailers to the standard.

The <u>Vehicle Certification Agency</u> does this in the UK.

There's no need to carry this certificate with the vehicle or trailer. But you may find it useful to either provide a copy of the certificate or other documentation so they can be shown to enforcement authorities at the roadside.

Some vehicles are tested to a higher standard than EN 12642 so that they can carry larger or unusual loads. In these cases, DVSA expects you to be able to show the relevant certificate at the roadside.

6.2 Double-deck trailers

Double-deck trailers are designed to optimise the available space in trailers. This reduces the carbon footprint and improves efficiency.

These benefits have led to an increase in their use over the last few years.

Risks assessments and securing solutions

Working at height can be problematic on any vehicle, however double decks present particular problems.

Operators and consignors (the person sending a shipment) should make sure that a thorough risk assessment has been carried out to identify the most practicable means of loading and securing goods on the vehicle.

Securing solutions are available to help to mitigate the risks of working at height on double deck trailers. For example, netting and strapping systems that attach to the trailer roof and can be pulled into place over the load and secured to the vehicle chassis from ground level allow goods to be secured without accessing the load bed.

Carrying palletised loads

Double deck trailers often carry palletised loads. Individual laden pallets are known as:

- 'light pallets' if they weigh up to 400kg

- 'heavy pallets' if they weight over 400kg

Don't use the upper deck for carrying stacked pallets or pallets weighing over 400kg.

Secure heavy pallets and stacked laden light pallets on the lower deck with rave to rave lashing or something similar.

Load securing on the upper deck
RHA, The Pallet Network (TPN) and the Association of Pallet Networks (APN) gave DVSA an acceptable solution on loading and securing for double-deck trailers:

Laden pallets on the upper deck of double-deck curtain-siders should be single-stacked; and weigh no more than 400kg each.

RHA, TPN, APN and enforcement bodies have agreed that the use of an extra internal curtain with integral straps designed to hug the load on the upper deck is a practicable means of mitigating the risks of falling objects during unloading and working at height.

This arrangement can be used by any operator or trailer manufacturer. It's recommended particularly for new trailers, but can also be fitted retrospectively.

The benefit of the internal curtain with integral straps is that it contains the pallets more effectively than using internal straps alone. This improves safety both on the road and in the workplace.

Load securing on the lower deck
Generally speaking loads carried on the lower deck and swan neck of a double-deck trailer should be secured as if they were carried on a single deck trailer.

Your risk assessment may indicate that for light goods or crushable loads it's practicable to use hanging straps or internal curtains on the lower deck.

Other methods of securing
This guidance is the minimum requirement needed to secure loads on existing double-deck trailers.

You can decide to use other methods of securing the load as well as those in this section, for example rated ratchet straps.

6.3 Rigid-sided vehicles

Vehicles with rigid sides are no different to any other vehicle when it comes to load securing. Load securing requirements still apply.

Gate-type systems

Most rigid-sided vehicles have a gate-type system. The security of the sides relies on 'locking' the sides to an anchor stanchion or stanchions fitted to the bed of the trailer.

These items must be kept in good condition. Any defects must be repaired at the earliest opportunity if the load securing relies on the sides of the vehicle.

Loads above the height of the sides

Loads stacked above the height of the sides of the vehicles need to be secured to the vehicle by other means – usually by over-the-top lashings. The sides of the vehicle can't be relied upon to secure this type of loading.

Loads above the height of a vehicles sides can affect stability and will raise the centre of gravity.

Load shift

Box vans and rigid-sided vehicles offer some load security, but you need to consider the effect of a load shift on vehicle stability. Goods carried in containers should also be secured to prevent movement during a journey.

Stop loose items from falling

Tarpaulins or netting/sheeting should be used on tippers, bulk containers and skips to stop loose items from falling.

Goods shouldn't be loaded over the height of the sides of the vehicle or skip.

6.4 Euroliner vehicles and trailers

Euroliner semi-trailers have an internal frame running down their length, usually hidden by standard curtain sides.

Different sized beams (made of aluminium or wood) can be placed in the frame, either lengthways – to strengthen the side – or across the width of the vehicle to separate the load.

The securing of light palletised goods – where each pallet or stack weigh no more than 400kg – on Euroline vehicles is accepted as sufficient when the these conditions are met:

- the load bed is filled to prevent the contents from moving when in transit

- the load is stacked against the headboard, or with any gap between the front of the load and the headboard packed to prevent it sliding forward

- the gap between the sides of the load and the frame/beams is less than 80 mm (approximately 3 inches)

- if the load doesn't reach the rear doors, then additional measures are in place to stop backward movement

- the beams and frame are in a serviceable condition, for example there are no cracks or obvious signs of damage, decay or rot

- the beams adequately contain the load so that there is no risk of items falling from the trailer when the curtains are pulled back - for example the load can't escape under, through or over the beams

Additional securing will be needed if:

- the vehicle is used to carry palletised or stacked loads which are more than 400kg

- the goods don't fill the load area – to prevent uncontrolled movement of the load under normal driving conditions

Additional securing could include rated lashing (heavy duty) straps attached between raves (hooks), or other approved methods.

7. Types of loads

In this section:

- **overview of vehicle stability**
- **light palletised goods**
- **roll cages**
- **crushable loads**
- **lightweight and fragile loads**
- **multi-drop or collection (diminishing loads)**
- **bulk loads carried loose**
- **equipment carried on vehicles**
- **skips**
- **flexible intermediate bulk containers (FIBCs)**
- **vehicle transporters**
- **drinks industry**
- **scaffolding equipment**
- **round timber**
- **steel, machinery and plant**

7.1 Overview of vehicle stability

The transport industry and the loads carried are extremely diverse, so it's very difficult to provide generic guidance on load securing that covers everything.

Many sectors of the industry have specific problems which require bespoke solutions to follow the DfT and EC guidelines.

DfT and EC guides

The DfT and EC guides do cover the vast majority of situations that you're likely to come across. They also include information on:

- the impact of the coefficient of friction (COF)

- how different materials move in relation to each other

- the number of straps required to overcome the effect of different COF values

What vehicle loading affects

How a vehicle is loaded can significantly affect:

- its handling on the road

- the likelihood of the load moving or becoming unstable during the journey

It's important to think about load distribution and load stability at the planning stage.

Centre of gravity

The centre of gravity of a loaded goods vehicle tends to be much higher than that of a passenger car. This makes a goods vehicle more likely to roll over than a car at the same speed.

Single items with a high centre of gravity (like large plant equipment) should be transported on low loaders to minimise the unbalancing effect.

Loads that move from side to side

Loads that are free to move from side to side within a vehicle can result in serious stability issues, even if the load is contained within the vehicle body.

The movement of live loads (like bagged sand or aggregate, hanging clothes or meat) can result in a 'pendulum' effect that quickly leads to vehicle rollover.

Rollcages

Rollcages can cause particular problems if they aren't secured.

There have been instances where cages have:

- rolled forward and punched through the headboard

- rolled backwards when the driver opens the rear doors for unloading

7.2 Light palletised goods

Pallets are widely used to carry all manner of goods, mainly because they are a safe and convenient way to store and move goods around via fork lift trucks.

Individual laden pallets are referred to as:

- 'light pallets' if they weigh up to 400kg

- 'heavy pallets' if they weight over 400kg

The goods on the pallets are often shrink-wrapped to restrict movement during transit. However, this wrapping doesn't provide any load securing.

Palletised loads must be stable and freestanding before any load securing is applied. Make sure goods are shrink-wrapped or banded to the pallet they're transported on. Otherwise, they could slide or topple off the pallet in transit or during unloading. Make sure that the unit load remains in a secure and stable condition at all times.

Transporting light palletised goods in curtained-sided vehicles

When deciding how to transport light palletised goods in curtain-sided vehicles, you should:

- think carefully about the most appropriate securing method for the load

- carry out a risk assessment that takes account of:

  - whether the load can be carried in a different body type

  - possible alternate securing methods that don't crush/damage the load

  - the risks of working at height when securing the load compared to the likely risks due to the load moving

You need to secure the load to reduce the risk of harm as far as is reasonably practicable.

Stacked light palletised goods

Stacked light palletised goods need to be secured in the same way as palletised goods over 400kg.

The best way is to use over-the-top lashings secured to the vehicle chassis or rave-to-rave.

Securing some products may present additional challenges, particularly if they're susceptible to strap damage (*see crushable loads*).

Light pallets on double-deck trailers

On double-deck trailers with inner curtains, light pallets should be carried on the top deck with heavier pallets or goods secured on the lower deck using over-the-top lashings.

Centre of gravity

Irrespective of the weight of a pallet, you should consider the centre of gravity.

Pallets with a high centre of gravity need extra strapping because of the potential for the load to be unstable, which increases the likelihood of movement during transit.

Loose items

Loose items (such as single pallets, pump trucks or chains) on flat beds need to be secured by other methods, as the internal strapping system or curtains will have no effect.

'Load hugging' curtains

Inner curtains tapered at the roof of the trailer are known as 'load hugging' curtains. These are used by some industries to secure the loads carried.

There will also be an outer curtain on these vehicles for weather protection as the inner curtains are constructed of nets and securing straps.

These vehicles and trailers are commonly found in the drinks industry and are covered extensively in the FTA guidance document (*see the drinks industry*).

7.3 Roll cages

Roll cages are frequently used to carry goods in all types of vehicles. These are becoming increasingly popular because they:

- make it easier to move goods around

- offer an element of security above that provided by pallets

Once loaded onto the vehicle they need securing to stop them from moving. This is often done using securing bars, lashings or other suitable methods.

Insecure roll cages can move around freely inside a vehicle load area. This can:

- have a significant impact on the vehicle's stability

- damage the goods

This is a particular problem with partially loaded vehicles (*see diminishing loads*) and presents further problems when unloading. You should take appropriate steps to stop movement of the roll cages to the side, front and particularly to rear.

To prevent goods being damaged care should be taken to stack products within the footprint of the cage. Damaging the goods can lead to the loads becoming loose and causing further problems when off loading.

7.4 Crushable loads

Goods that could be damaged by rave-to-rave over-the-top lashings can be protected by using:

- corner boards

- edge protectors

- wide strapping systems

These spread the load to allow the load to be secured to the vehicle bed.

Crushable loads could need extra protection (like shrink-wrap or other packaging) to be protected enough to be transported. Netting systems (with straps interwoven through the netting) can be used for these loads.

Other methods or other vehicle types may need to be considered for crushable loads.

7.5 Lightweight and fragile loads

There are some loads which are very unlikely to cause any load securing problems while in transit in curtain side vehicles, for example, small amounts of polystyrene insulation.

It's still important that the load is stopped from moving due to the danger to the person responsible for unloading the vehicle.

You might not be able to use traditional lashings because of the damage they would cause. However, internal straps may retain the load sufficiently dependant on the size of the objects.

You could also use some sort of internal frame or roll cage to provide the necessary securing. Make sure the frame itself is secure if you use this method

7.6 Multi-drop or collection (diminishing loads)

The DfT code of practice requires 50% of the load to be secured to prevent rearward and sideways movement.

When an entire load is delivered in one drop using the appropriate securing, it's quite straight forward. However, this becomes more difficult for vehicles involved in multi-drops or carrying diminishing loads.

Multi-site deliveries can cause issues with responsibility for the safety of the load.

Plan for the diminishing load

Diminishing loads should be accounted for at the planning stage.

You should develop a clear system of work and communicate it to all parties so there's no misunderstanding about what should be done at each delivery.

Having enough appropriate securing

Dependant upon the type of vehicle used, parts of the load will either be removed from:

- the side when using curtain-sided vehicles

- the rear with rigid-sided vehicles

- both from a flat bed

So it's important that the driver has enough appropriate securing with them to be able to fix the problems caused by diminishing loads.

Load the vehicle correctly

The whole process can be made much easier if the vehicle is loaded correctly in the first place.

If the load is removed in a hap-hazard way, gaps may appear that could be detrimental to effectiveness of the load securing system. If this happens, the driver might find it easier to use dunnage or blocking to fill the gaps, and keep the integrity of the original security.

Reload the vehicle

The other way to keep safe would be to reload the vehicle and reapply the chosen securing.

This shows why it's important to plan properly, load the vehicle correctly and make sure the driver has enough load securing equipment.

Diminishing load from the rear

A diminishing load from the rear causes extra problems, as the rear of the trailer won't provide any security once the rearmost part of the load has been removed.

Loads can be secured by cross over straps, kites or sails to comply with the 50% requirement. The strapping needs to be maintained as the load diminishes or an intermediate bulkhead could be used.

Watch out for overloading

Drivers should be wary about axle overloads when removing large portions of the load from either the front or the rear. The remaining load may well need re-distribution to avoid these situations.

7.7 Bulk loads carried loose

You should carry loads like wood chippings, pellets and grain in solid-sided vehicles and curtain-sided vehicles specifically adapted for that use. These vehicles have additional strapping and covering to secure the load within the vehicle.

The likelihood of such items becoming insecure is unlikely if carried in a covered secure containing trailer.

Grain carriers and vehicles servicing the wood processing industry will have this type of vehicle. Most will have a blowing system fitted to the vehicle to load and unload the vehicle contents into a storage unit.

Standard curtain-sided trailers shouldn't be used for this kind of load.

7.8 Equipment carried on vehicles

Equipment carried on vehicles (like Hiabs, fork lift trucks and pallet pump trucks) should be properly secured when not in use.

Lorry-mounted cranes (Hiabs)

Hiabs should be deactivated and correctly seated and not used as part of the load securing system.

Pallet pump trucks

Pallet pump trucks should be secured in the same way as the rest of a vehicles load, for example with lashings or other suitable methods.

Lorry-mounted fork list truck

Lorry-mounted fork lift trucks (often called 'moffetts') should be secured using the manufacture's recommended instructions.

Rear-mounted forklift truck.

7.9 Skips

Empty or loaded skips can be carried on either:

- dedicated skip lorries
- flatbed vehicles

It's recommended that skips are carried on skip lorries wherever possible, as it can be very difficult to adequately secure a skip on a flatbed vehicle.

Loaded or partly-loaded skips

Loaded or partly-loaded skips shouldn't be stacked on top of each other for transport, even on a dedicated skip lorry.

The lower skip doesn't provide a stable base and there is a risk of the upper skip/skips moving under sudden braking, or falling from the side of the vehicle under a combined steering and braking manoeuvre (for example, swerving to avoid another road user).

Skips

Loaded or partly-loaded skips should not be stacked or top of each other for transport.

Lifting arms

Some skip lorries have a shaft connecting the upper ends of the lifting arms. This is used by some operators to 'press down' on stacked skips. This isn't recommended. Using the lifting arms for load restraint can lead to fatigue, which could lead to cracking in the lifting arms.

Fatigue cracks can grow very slowly and the lifting arms will still operate normally. Eventually the crack will grow to the extent that there's no longer enough strength in the arm to hold the weight of a skip, and sudden and unexpected failure of the lifting arm may occur.

The lifting arms of skip lorries should be inspected every 12 months by a competent person in order to comply with the Lifting Operations and Lifting Equipment Regulations 1998 (LOLER).

Some types of lifting equipment have a connecting beam between the two hydraulic lifting arms. In certain situations, this beam can be used to secure two loaded skips.

Tests show that when two loaded skips are carried on the vehicle and the hydraulic rams are pushing the bar down onto the top skip, then enough pressure is applied.

DVSA will accept this as providing acceptable security when these conditions are met:

- the lifting equipment is in good condition and tested to LOLER regulations

- there's a connecting beam between the two lifting arms and it's in contact with the top skip at both sides

- the bottom of the top skip is at least 100 millimetres below the top of the bottom skip

- loose loads are sheeted or covered properly

- if skips are carried in a line, then loaded skips are only at the rear of the vehicle where the hydraulic lifting arms and beams secure the load

- you can produce evidence at the roadside that the vehicle has been tested at TRL (Transport Research Laboratory) or a similar facility

- the chains used to lift the skips are attached for extra security

7.10 Flexible intermediate bulk containers (FIBCs)

FIBCs, sacks and other bulk bags can become unstable during transport due to the loads settling. This could put the driver or anyone else unloading the vehicle at risk.

The most appropriate vehicle for this type of load would be a rigid-sided vehicle with securing supplemented by lashings.

Drop-side vehicles

When using drop-side vehicles, make sure the tail boards, hinges and any fastening mechanisms are in good condition.

You might also need to consider additional security if the load is higher than the side of the vehicle. Also consider using tarpaulins to prevent any loose loads being blown from the FIBCs.

Flat bed vehicles

These loads should be loaded to the headboard if they're carried on flat bed vehicles. To stop movement to the side, use lashing straps with edging strips or some other method to disperse the pressure from the strap onto the load.

Tarpaulins rated for load securing with inter woven rated straps can also be used to provide effective security. Due to the nature of the load it is good practice to check for movement during a journey.

Curtained-sided vehicles

FIBCs carried in curtain-sided vehicle present similar problems and should be secured in the same way.

Other load securing solutions are also available which would be effective for FIBC such as wide straps suspended on bungee cord.

Open or unsealed FIBCs

You may need to put extra sheeting or tarpaulin over the top of the load to stop products from escaping the FIBC if they're not sealed or closed.

Roping and sheeting

Roping and sheeting, used correctly, and using equipment in good condition, can be an effective way of securing FIBCs to meet the requirements of UK and European standards.

DVSA recommends that you use rope and sheets that have been strength tested and rated. This is so you can easily prove that the load is secured to enforcement authorities at the roadside.

The sheet should also fully contain the load, rather than resting on top of it.

Damaged or torn sheets, and frayed or worn ropes, should be replaced or repaired.

7.11 Vehicle transporters

You can move vehicles and plant equipment on specialised vehicles like:

- car transporters

- flatbed vehicles

- low loaders

Moving cars and light vans up to 3,500kg on car transporters

Vehicles carried on car transporters should face forward, unless the loading scheme says otherwise.

Their weight should be distributed evenly across the width of the vehicle so the driver has enough space to work safely on either side.

Their centre of gravity should be over the lengthwise centre line of the transporter.

When loading, follow the manufacturer's recommendations. The parking brake should always be on after a vehicle's loaded.

Car transporters have a high centre of gravity compared to many other types of goods vehicles. To reduce the risk of rollover, the heavier vehicles should be on the lower deck.

Use extra securing to prevent movement in transit. Securing is generally achieved through a mixture of blocking/chocking and webbing lashings.

The number of chocks and lashings used depends on the load. But as a general guide, there should be three points of contact between the vehicle and the transporter.

vehicle on flat deck	2 wheels secured by lashings, preferably diagonally opposite, plus one chock or lashing on a third wheel of each vehicle
vehicle on angled deck	3 wheels secured, 2 with lashings and one with chocks, or 3 with lashings
first and last vehicles on decks	4 wheels secured by lashings on vehicles loaded at the front and rear

If it's impractical to use chocks for some vehicles on a transporter, an extra wheel can be secured with a lashing strap.

Regularly inspect the check plate for wear and tear.

Some vehicle manufactures recommend that each wheel should be attached. You're encouraged to follow this advice.

Lashings used to secure vehicles should be:

- manufactured to the BS EN 12195-2 Standard

- be rated for at least 1,500 daN

- in a serviceable condition without obvious defects that would affect the strength of the lashing

Lashings should ideally pass over the wheel lengthways to hold the wheel down to the load bed.

The lashings should be attached to either dedicated attachment points or to dedicated attachment eyes fitted to the transporter or floor attachment points, as long they're in a serviceable condition. Ratchets should be closed and locked.

If you use wheel chocks, they should be placed so that they aid load security by securing against:

- the braking force on a flat deck

- gravity on an angled deck

Cars and light vans up to 3,500kg transported on flatbed or curtain-sided trailers.

Flatbed trailers don't have a superstructure to stop unintended load movement. Because of this more securing is needed.

Load vehicles as close to the headboard as possible, with the parking brake on.

vehicle on standard flatbed	all four wheels secured with lashings: chocks on at least two wheels, preferably diagonally opposite
vehicle on recovery transporter trailer	winch cable attached, plus lashings on at least two wheels, preferably diagonally opposite

If the design of the transporting vehicle makes it difficult to secure the wheels, use extra lashings.

Stacked scrap vehicles should be stable without lashings.

To stop the webbing being damaged by sharp edges, use webbing sleeves or something similar to protect any lashings passing over the stack.

Lashings used to secure vehicles should be:

- manufactured to the BS EN 12195-2 Standard

- rated for at least 1,500 daN

- in good condition without obvious defects that would affect their strength

The superstructure and curtains of a standard curtain-sided trailer aren't enough to provide load restraint for a vehicle. The vehicle must be secured as if it was being transported on a flatbed trailer.

A trailer constructed to the BS EN 12642-XL standard may provide some containment. But an XL trailer alone isn't enough to prevent load movement. The reinforced body structure should be thought of as an extra safety measure rather than part of the load securing system.

Vehicles should be loaded as close to the headboard as possible – with the parking brake on – and chocked and lashed.

Transporting vehicles over 3,500 kg on car transporters
Generally, there should be four points of contact between the vehicle and the transporter, consisting of either:

- two chocks and two lashing straps – preferably on diagonally opposing wheels

- one chock and three lashing straps

- four lashing straps, one on each wheel

Transporting vehicles over 3,500 kg on flatbed trailers
Ideally, vehicles over 3,500 kg should be moved on low loader trailers so that the centre of gravity is as low as possible.

A high centre of gravity can affect the stability of the transporting vehicle and increase the risk of rollover or loss of control.

There should be four points of contact between the vehicle and the trailer, in the form of lashing straps on each wheel.

Chocks can be used for extra safety but shouldn't be considered part of the load securing system.

Vehicles should be loaded to the headboard with the parking brake on and the vehicle left in gear if possible.

Heavy goods vehicles

Ideally, tractor units and trailers should be moved on low loaders so that the centre of gravity is kept as low as possible. This helps to reduce the risk of rollover or loss of control.

Secure vehicles using a lashing system to prevent unintended movement. Chains are preferable.

The parking brake must be on and the wheels chocked or otherwise prevented from movement. For example, by placing the vehicle up against the swan neck.

Vehicles should be lashed using direct lashing. This means, one attached to the vehicle, and the other to the transporting low loader or flatbed.

There should be at least four lashings, secured as part of two opposing pairs. The angle of the straps or chains relative to the load bed should be as close to horizontal as possible.

Extra frictional lashing – up and over the load – using webbing straps can be used to increase the safety of the load.

If the vehicle has attachment points, use these for load securing. Also, attach lashings to rated attachment points on the low loader or flatbed load bed wherever possible.

Lashings shouldn't be attached to sheeting hooks, as these aren't strong enough to withstand the required forces.

If more than one trailer is carried by piggy-back, each trailer should be lashed to the trailer it's carried on, and then to the transporting vehicle.

Carrying by 'piggyback'

Carrying vehicles by 'piggyback' can significantly reduce the stability of the transporting vehicle.

Plant equipment

Heavy-wheeled plant should ideally be moved on low loaders so that the centre of gravity is kept as low as possible. This helps to reduce the risk of rollover or loss of control.

Secure vehicles using a lashing system to prevent unintended movement. Chains are preferable.

There should be at least four lashings, secured as part of two opposing pairs. The angle of the straps or chains relative to the load bed should be as close to horizontal as possible.

Extra frictional lashing – up and over the load – using webbing straps can be used to increase the safety of the load.

If the vehicle has attachment points, use these for load securing. Also, attach lashings to rated attachment points on the low loader or flatbed load bed wherever possible.

Lashings shouldn't be attached to sheeting hooks, as these aren't strong enough to withstand the required forces.

Ideally, vehicles should be loaded against the swan neck of a low loader or the headboard of a flatbed. This creates a physical barrier to movement besides the lashing system.

Chocks or lateral timbers can also help to prevent movement. Booms, jibs, buckets, grabs and other components should be separately secured to the transporting vehicle with one or more lashing.

Don't rely on hydraulic pressure or any other form of stored energy to prevent movement.

There's very specific guidance on securing plant vehicles in the DfT code of practice. You should bear in mind the rules contained in the *Construction* and *Use Regulations* about the maximum dimensions when any equipment is extended to the front or rear of the vehicle.

Scrap metal

Scrap metal, including scrap cars, should be transported with care. It's a high-density load and may contain sharp edges that can cut through webbing lashings.

It's recommended that you use chain lashings for this type of load.

The friction between the load and the vehicle load bed is likely to be very low so it's important to use an adequate number of lashings.

7.12 Drinks industry

Kegs and barrels should be secured to:

- prevent them moving while the vehicle is in motion

- reduce the risk of them falling out of the vehicle during unloading

This is very important for kerbside deliveries to smaller premises where pedestrians are at risk of being hit.

Lashing loads to multi-drop kerbside delivery sites may put the driver at more risk. Other restraint methods should be used if possible.

You should transport small and/or breakable items in stillages if no other method can be used.

7.13 Scaffolding equipment

Scaffolding equipment will comprise of poles, boards and ancillary equipment, and is often transported on flatbed vehicles.

Scaffolding equipment should be loaded so that it doesn't move relative to the vehicle under normal driving conditions. Fold-up sides and a rear gate or sail can:

- help to prevent load movement

- allow equipment to be transported without lashings as long as the load isn't stacked higher than the sides

The load should be placed in contact with the headboard if possible. If a gap is left, an intermediate bulkhead (which can be constructed from scaffold boards), blocking or dunnage can be used to prevent movement, or lashings can be used over the load.

Groups of poles should be 'belly wrapped' and secured to prevent movement during the journey.

7.14 Round timber

Round timber is normally carried on a skeleton type trailers with goal posts. This is allowed as long as the goal posts are in good condition and are secure.

As a minimum, each pair of goal posts should be accompanied by over-the-top lashing, either straps or chains, from chassis to chassis.

7.15 Steel, machinery and plant

Chains are used for heavy loads like steel, machinery and plant equipment.

Steel is a high-density, high-risk load. The consequences of load shift can be extremely serious.

Movement of the load endangers:

- the driver - if the load slides forward during the journey or shifts sideways and causes the driver to lose control of his vehicle

- other road users and pedestrians - if the load shifts sideways or slides backwards and falls off the vehicle

- unloading personnel - if the load has become unstable during the journey and collapses during unloading

It is very important to load steel so that they are stable on the vehicle without relying on lashings. This may mean using chocks or blocking to make sure the load is stable.

Even though steel is heavy, don't rely on the weight of the load alone to hold it in place.

The friction between individual items in the load, and between the load and the load bed, can be very low – particularly for painted or coated products and cold rolled products.

If the vehicle is loaded in an uncovered area, wet or icy weather conditions can also reduce the positive effect of friction.

Loading against the headboard

Steel should be loaded so that it is against the headboard of the vehicle if possible.

Loading to the headboard also means that the:

- headboard can be considered part of the load securing system

- minimum number of lashings needed will be less than for a load loaded away from the headboard

The headboard should be strong enough to prevent the load moving.

If the load comes through the headboard it will go into the driver's cab, the headboard is critical in protecting the driver. For the same reason, the load shouldn't be loaded above the height of the headboard unless precautions have been taken to stop it sliding forward.

Securing with chain lashings

The load should be secured with chain lashings when it's loaded.

It's very important to make sure that all parts of the load are secured. Building the load into a 'pyramid' shape can help to:

- make sure that the lashings are in contact with the whole load

- stop individual items sliding or toppling

Belly-wrapping is particularly useful in securing bundled products.

Chain lashings are very effective in restraining steel and aren't damaged by sharp edges like webbing lashings. If any webbing is used, it should be protected from any sharp edges by using either:

- webbing sleeves

- edge protectors on the load

Side posts or side boards help to protect both other road users and unloading personnel. They're a useful way of making sure the load doesn't endanger anyone if the lashing system fails for any reason.

Steel loaded correctly

Chain lashings are very effective in restraining steel an are not damaged by sharp edges like webbing lashings.

Unloading steel

Steel can be unloaded by fork lift truck or by crane.

Avoid anyone standing on the load bed during unloading. If this can't be avoided, you need to think carefully about:

- where they should stand

- communication with the fork lift truck driver or crane operator

- whether they need fall arrest equipment

8. Load securing solutions

In this section:

- **overview of load securing solutions**

- **securing equipment**

- **headboards and bulk head**

- **rope hooks**

8.1 Overview of load securing solutions

Since the DVSA and <u>Health and Safety Laboratory</u> initiative on load securing there has been a large increase in the number of load securing solutions available.

These range from systems which reduce the risk of working at height including lashings suspended from bungee cords to specially designed extendable poles used to help the driver.

The following have also become more readily available:

- wider lashings

- kites

- sails

- friction mats

- edge protectors

All of these are valuable tools to help you secure awkward loads to vehicles to reduce the risk of load movements and associated road safety problems.

8.2 Securing equipment

All equipment used to secure a load to a vehicle should be in a good serviceable condition.

Damage to securing equipment

Damage to the equipment should be reported and the equipment replaced as soon as reasonably practicable.

Spare equipment

Spare equipment should be carried to allow the driver to:

- supplement the load securing if required

- replace any lashings which have become damaged during transit or where a third party has secured a load inadequately

Inspecting equipment

You should regularly inspect the state of the vehicle headboard or any other internal bulk head (if used).

Curtains should be inspected and where rips are identified they should be repaired as these will compromise the curtains ability to contain a load should a load shift occur.

Equipment not in use

When not in use, the equipment should be stored safely or secured to prevent it falling from the vehicle during transit.

8.3 Headboards and bulk head

The DfT code of practice requires that the load securing systems used should be able to withstand a force not less than 100% of the load to the front.

Generally, but not exclusively, vehicles will rely on a headboard/bulk head or intermediate bulk head to provide this security.

Inspect the headboard regularly

You should regularly inspect the headboard to make sure it's in good condition.

Different types of headboard

Different vehicles have different types of headboard and not all are suitable to retain 100% of the load. You should make sure that the headboard fitted to your vehicle is strong enough for the load being carried.

Put loads as close to the headboard as possible

To take the full advantage of the bulkhead/headboards loads should be located as close to the bulkhead as possible.

However this might not always be possible due to the potential for exceeding weights or due to the nature of the load itself.

Fill the gap between the load and headboard

In situations where the load isn't located up to the headboard then ideally suitable blocking or dunnage should be used to fill the gap.

The type of blocking used will be dictated by the load carried and the size of the gap, for example the larger the gap the more robust the blocking would need to be.

In some circumstances it would be appropriate to use additional lashings to secure the load rather than blocking.

Height of the load

Another issue to consider is the height of the load in relation to the height of the headboard.

Where a vehicle is laden with a large indivisible load the headboard can provide support as long as the load can't topple over the height of the headboard.

If the load could topple over the headboard then additional securing will be required, such as cross strapping to the front, if indeed the chosen vehicle is suitable for the load.

Items above the headboard

Individual items which are above the headboard (such as scaffolding pipes or large wooden planks) will need either:

- extra suitable securing to increase the down force

- an intermediate bulkhead

8.4 Rope hooks

Rope hooks are for securing sheeting to the vehicle, with ropes or nets attached to protect the load from the weather.

They shouldn't be used as an anchor point to secure over-the-top straps or chains.

Drivers who have traditionally 'roped and sheeted' a load using the 'klinch' or 'drivers' knot can use the rope hooks to secure the load to the vehicle if this system is sufficient to do so.

Many drivers don't have the knowledge or ability to rope and sheet as more effective systems have become available.

Check ropes regularly

The ropes should be:

- rated and marked as such

- inspected regularly to identify any damage

Ropes showing signs of wear should be replaced at the earliest opportunity.

Over-the-top lashings

Over-the-top lashings should never be attached to the rope hooks. The tensioning of the lashings could:

- damage the hooks

- cause the load to become insecure

Lashing straps should attach either directly to the vehicle chassis or rave.

Chapter **28**
Advice for Passing LGV Driving Test

Choosing a Training School: Considerations

Avoid brokers at all costs-they will take your money and deliver as little as possible. They often say that they have 30 plus training centres around the country. No genuine trainer has and so they are easy to spot.

It's also important to bear in mind that there are some poor training schools out there.

Questions to keep in mind:

- Training schools reputation? Check them out thoroughly, do your research and try to find some genuine reviews before making any payment. Gaining an LGV licence is an expensive undertaking – choosing the wrong school could be a costly mistake.

- Do they offer one-on-one training or is it two learner drivers being taught in one truck at the same time? There is twice the hands-on driving experience if it's one-on-one!

- Can you take an assessment drive?

- What is their average pass rate?

- Can you visit the school?

- Are the vehicles in good condition?

- Lesson duration?

- Do the instructors have the DVSA (Driving Standards Agency) qualification? Note: this is a voluntary qualification, not mandatory.

- Which LGV test centre do they use?

Five day intensive courses.

Intensive courses allow trainees to distance themselves from other life distractions and to become fully immersed in the training. On an intensive course, it is possible to lose concentration and to start making mistakes during one of the five consecutive days. This may or may not happen. If it does, do not lose confidence, it is perfectly natural, the mind will only focus intensely for a certain period of time before wandering. Concentration will and always does return.

About Your Practical Test

What to Expect …

You must bring your photocard driving licence. If you don't have your photocard driving licence then your paper licence and a valid passport will suffice.

Your test will be cancelled and you'll lose your fee if you don't bring these on the day.

Ideally take a 40 minute pre-test lesson, then arrive at the test centre about 15 minutes prior to your test, so that you're not hurried or waiting for too long.

Remember to switch off your mobile phone and any other personal distractions.

Your practical test will last about 1 hour 30 minutes and includes:

- Practical road driving

- Off-road exercises

- Vehicle safety questions

- 10 minutes of independent driving during which your examiner will ask you to follow signs or follow directions to reach a destination.

Practical road driving – during this, exercise your examiner will assess your ability to operate, control the vehicle and carry out various tasks. These include:

- Moving off from a stationary position, checking mirrors and blind spot.

- Use of the vehicle controls

- Move away at an angle, uphill and downhill

- Do a controlled stop

- Use the mirrors

- Give appropriate signals

- Show awareness and anticipation of other road users' intentions.

- Manage your progress and control your vehicle speed.

- Deal with hazards

- Select a safe space to stop.

The off road exercises will include:

- An 'S' shaped reverse into a bay.

- Follow your instructor's advice and fix a reversing marker to the rear mud guard of the truck. This will help get the truck aligned into the designated box.

- Taking your seat belt off just prior to carrying out the reversing exercise may make the manoeuver easier. Remember to fasten your seat belt immediately after the exercise is complete.

- You can take up to 2 shunts for the reversing exercise if required.

- You are permitted to get out of the vehicle once

- so make good use of the first shunt to ensure the rear of the truck is close to or in place.

- Also demonstrating the uncoupling and re-coupling procedure if you're taking a test with a trailer.

You can still pass your practical test with up to 15 minor faults. In the event of a mistake, simply move on and do not dwell on it.

Lorry and bus 'show me, tell me' vehicle safety questions

1. About the questions

You'll be asked some vehicle safety questions during your test for one of these categories of licence:

- C1 – Medium sized lorry
- C – Large goods lorry
- D1 – Minibus
- D – Bus and coach

- C1+E – Medium sized lorry with trailer
- C+E – Large goods lorry with trailer
- D1+E – Minibus with trailer
- D+E – Bus and coach with trailer

The questions ...

2.1 Show me how you would check that all doors including cargo doors are secure.

All doors must be closed and locking levers for cargo doors are set in the recommended secured position.

2.2 Show me how you would check for air leaks on this vehicle.

Charge the air tanks, consult gauges for drops in air pressure. Walk round vehicle listening for any obvious leaks.

2.3 Tell me the main safety factors involved in loading this vehicle.

The load should be evenly distributed throughout the length of the vehicle so as not to affect control while the vehicle is being driven. Any load must be carried so that it does not endanger other road users. It must be securely stowed within the size and weight limits for the vehicle. The load needs to be secure so that it cannot move or fall from the vehicle when cornering or braking.

2.4 Tell me how you would check the condition of the reflectors on this vehicle.

Ensure that all reflectors are fitted, clean, and functional (not cracked or broken).

2.5 Tell me how you would check the condition of the windscreen and windows on this vehicle.

The windscreen and windows must be clean, clear and free from defects. No mascots or sticker that restrict view.

2.6 Show me how you would check the condition of the mudguards on this vehicle.

As part of daily walk-round check ensure mudguards and spray suppression equipment are secure.

2.7 Tell me how you would check your tyres to ensure that they are correctly inflated, have sufficient tread depth and that their general condition is safe to use on the road.

Follow manufacturer's guide, using appropriate equipment, check and adjust pressures when tyres are cold. Must have a tread depth of at least 1mm across ¾ of the breadth of the tread and in a continuous band around the entire circumference. There should be no cuts, damage or signs of cord visible at the sidewalls.

2.8 Tell me how you would check the condition of the windscreen wipers on this vehicle.

Windscreen wipers must operate. Blades should be in good condition.

2.9 Tell me how you would check the condition of the body is safe on this vehicle.

As part of a daily walk-round check, ensure the body is fully roadworthy and there are no significant defects. No loose panels or items, which could endanger other road users. All inspection panels must be secure.

2.10 Show me how you would check for the correct air pressure on this vehicle.

Ensure gauges are reading the correct pressures for the vehicle and that all warning lights are extinguished and audible warning devices are not sounding.

2.11 Identify where you would check the engine oil level and tell me how you would check that the engine has sufficient oil.

Identify dipstick/oil level indicator, describe check of oil level against the minimum/maximum markers.

2.12 Show me how you would check the wheel nuts are secure on this vehicle.

A visual check to identify any nuts that are obviously loose, and check that the wheel nut indicators (if fitted) are in alignment.

2.13 Show me how you would check the operation (specify horn, warning device for reversing) of the audible warning devices on this vehicle.

Demonstrate use of control.

2.14 Tell me how you would check the condition of the suspension on this vehicle.

As part of a daily walk-round check, suspension should be checked for any obvious signs of deterioration or damage.

2.15 Show me how you would check that the brake lights are working on this vehicle (I can assist you, if you need to switch the ignition on, please don't start the engine).

Operate brake pedal, make use of reflections in windows, garage doors, etc, or ask someone to help.

2.16 Identify where you would check the engine coolant level and tell me how you would check that the engine has the correct level.

Identify high/low level markings on header tank where fitted or radiator filler cap, and describe how to top up to correct level.

2.17 Tell me how you would check that the headlamps, sidelights and tail lights are working.

Explain: Operate switch (turn on ignition if necessary), walk round vehicle.

2.18 Show me how you would replace the tachograph disc on this vehicle.

Candidate to demonstrate how to insert tachograph disc. Digital tachographs may require an explanation if the candidate does not have a digital card.

2.19 Tell me how you would operate the loading mechanism on this vehicle (vehicle specific i.e. tail lift).

Candidates should be able to explain briefly the correct operation and safe working practice of specific machinery fitted to the vehicle, eg tail lift, kneeling bus.

2.20 Show me / explain how you would check that the power assisted steering is working.

If the steering becomes heavy the system may not be working properly. Before starting a journey two simple checks can be made. Gentle pressure on the steering wheel, maintained while the engine is started, should result in a slight but noticeable movement as the system begins to operate. Alternatively turning the steering wheel just after moving off will give an immediate indication that the power assistance is functioning.

2.21 Show me how you would check that the direction indicators are working.

Applying the indicators or hazard warning switch and check functioning of all indicators.

2.22 Identify where the windscreen washer reservoir is and tell me how you would check the windscreen washer level.

Identify reservoir and explain how to check level.

2.23 Show me what instrument checks you would make before and after starting the engine on this vehicle.

Check to make sure all gauges and warning systems are working. Ensure that all gauges are reading correctly and that warning lights / audible warning devices are extinguished before moving away.

2.24 Show me where the first aid equipment is kept on this vehicle.

Candidate to indicate equipment if carried. Where equipment is not present, candidates should be able to explain under what circumstances (ie vehicle types, loads carried) it must be provided.

2.25 Show me how you would clean the windscreen using the windscreen washer and wipers.

Operate control to wash and wipe windscreen (turn ignition on if necessary).

2.26 Show me how you would set the windscreen demister to clear the windows effectively.

Set all relevant controls including; fan, temperature, air direction / source and heated screen to clear windscreen and windows. Engine does not have to be started for this demonstration.

2.27 Show me how you would switch on the rear fog light(s) and explain when you would use it/them (no need to exit vehicle).

Operate switch (turn on ignition and dipped headlights if necessary). Check warning light is on. Explain use.

2.28 Show me how you switch your headlight from dipped to main beam.

Operate switch (with ignition or engine on if necessary), check with main beam warning light.

After you've taken the practical test your examiner will tell you if you've passed or failed and explain how you did overall.

You'll pass your test if you make:

- 15 or less minor faults.

- No serious or dangerous faults.

If you fail, you can book another driving test straight away, but you can't take it for another 3 clear working days.

Useful contacts for learners:

- Booking your theory test (https://www.gov.uk/book-theory-test)

- Book your driving test (https://www.gov.uk/book-driving-test)

- In the case of your test being cancelled by the DVSA at short notice you can apply for a refund of expenses here (https://www.gov.uk/government/publications/application-for-refunding-out-of-pocket-expenses)

Psychology – The examiner and you

The examiner is likely to be from an ex-police or military background. These people take dangerous vehicles and their personal role in public safety very seriously. To gain their confidence, a demonstration of the following is necessary:

- Competence, ability to keep the vehicle fully under control at all times.

- Anticipation, forward thinking, awareness of all road users and of possible hazards ahead of time.

- Road positioning, choosing the correct lane at the correct time/taking up two lanes where necessary.

Driver's Attitude

A good attitude, responsible and confident.

Note

Ex-forces people often mix socially with people of similar experience and not more alternative types. Due to negative media stereotyping, an unconscious misunderstanding of more alternative people can sometimes occur.

With this in mind: If you are alternative looking, to gain respect and not to be misunderstood, it may be worth considering being a bit conformist for a few hours. Achieved simply by doing what is necessary not to stand out. One thing is for sure they will not change for you.

Note

I do not believe in discrimination of any kind.

My Test

I included this section on my test experience for information purposes only-it's not an exercise in tutoring or self indulgence. My hope was simply that including this might help in what I know is a very tough, expensive and vital challenge when trying to get into this industry.

I took an intensive five day LGV 1 training course in Bristol. The trainer was Ex Military and used a stick to jab me in the ribs if I made a mistake. The idea being if I repeated the same mistake I would connect it with those jabs and remember. I would say this technique worked.

I took 1 to 1 training which provided more hands on driving time. I knuckled down and focussed hard. The first three days really went well and my confidence grew. That was until the mock test on the 4th day. On that day, I couldn't do anything right. I bounced off curbs, pulled out on cars at junctions and messed up on the reversing. My confidence started to crash. The instructor was a good man and he told me that during his career he'd seen this happen many times before. It was just the mind letting go for a day after intensively focussing for long periods and that my concentration would return.

The Day of the Test

I had a very poor night's sleep. I was tired. Knowing that I would need to be fully awake and alert on the test I had a very strong coffee. It didn't help my nerves but totally woke me up. Fortunately on the pre-drive lesson to the test centre I found that my focus had fully returned.

During the day I incurred five main problems on the drive:

- **Focus.** My trainer had taught me a seven second rule of checking the mirrors including actually turning my head slightly to demonstrate to the examiner that I was doing so. This necessary but constant distraction made concentrating on all other aspects of the test very difficult indeed.

- **Hesitancy.** On approaching a busy roundabout with oncoming traffic, I couldn't assess whether the gaps between vehicles were quite big enough for me to be able to pull out.

- **Random.** I encountered a group of schoolchildren who, on seeing me coming, decided it would be a good idea to wind me up by wandering in and out of the road in front of the truck. They continued to do this for at least a minute or two, by this time my blood pressure was going through the roof (I thought to myself, bless them because the children are our future. Not really, if the examiner hadn't been there and I had a shotgun, things would have been a very different :-)

- **Knowing the route.** At a short distance ahead I could see a few people waiting to cross a pedestrian crossing. I didn't know if they had pushed the button, all I knew was that the lights were showing no sign of changing. The road ahead of me was clear but I had to make a decision to accelerate or just go on very steadily. My decision was to just crawl up to the lights. Just as I arrived the lights suddenly changed to red, even at this low speed, I had to stop sharply, at that moment the examiner slammed his clipboard down hard onto the dashboard, as if to make out I'd almost sent him through the windscreen (didn't do my nerves much good).

- I was driving down a busy but narrow road. It had parked cars along both sides and I had to make a decision to commit to going through-I knew if I met another large vehicle it would be impossible to pass. Just as I committed I saw a bin lorry oncoming in the distance. Luckily the driver may have guessed there was a test going on and kindly stopped to let me through.

Summary

Focus. I pushed myself to get into the zone, told myself only to think about the test itself and dismiss all thoughts of the past or future. "Pass or fail, money, I'll worry about that when I've finished". Some thoughts did arise and I just ignored them.

Hesitancy. I displayed hesitancy at the busy roundabout and pedestrian crossing. At the time I had no doubt that if I obstructed and caused another vehicle to slow down and alter their course that this would be an instant fail. If I'd gone through the red light I'd also have failed. Whereas to err on the side of caution and try to keep the truck wheels rolling and use up some possible hesitancy points, would be at least a possible pass if the rest of the drive went well.

Knowing the route was a big key. Because I knew the roads the constant mirror checking wasn't as big an issue, as it could have been. Other advantages were: pre-knowing speed limits, tight turns, awkward obstacles, traffic light systems, steep hills, narrow roads etc.

Random. Kids and bin lorry experience. These events were completely out of my control. I was very fortunate that on the day things went my way. I understand the test pass rate is 33%, as one in three people pass first time. This shows the level of difficulty and things that can happen on the day to affect the outcome. Whatever you do, try not to go through the whole test and then fail on the Highway Code questions!! Examiners see this part of the test as equally important.

Note

In my experience coffee did help with alertness but I wouldn't recommend it to a non coffee drinker.

Examiners Assessment Criteria

There are three main types of fault recorded. Minor, serious and dangerous.

Minor Faults. Examples: undue hesitancy, gear crunching, insufficient use of mirrors, insufficient road progress etc.

When a driver makes a mistake a fault is noted down on the examiners test report in the relevant section.

If the driver commits the same mistake again it will be noted again in the same section. Same mistake a third time the examiner can and probably will change the fault from minor to serious.

To Summarise. If a driver has 15 points to play with and they make a few small errors which are noted in various sections of the test sheet, they will probably pass. If they make three of the same errors they could well fail.

Serious Faults. Examples. Pulling out in front of another vehicle causing it to alter course. Truck or trailer mounting the curb, going through a red light at a crossing, etc. The likelihood of a driver failing their test after committing one or more serious faults is extremely high.

Dangerous Faults. Examples include: going the wrong way down a one-way road, almost hitting a pedestrian, colliding with another vehicle etc. A dangerous fault is an immediate fail.

Researched Most Common Test Mistakes, Faults/Fails

Response to signs and road markings

- Driving unnecessarily over central dividing line.

- Not correctly following lane directional arrows

- Stopping inside a yellow box junction when the exit is not clear (unless turning).

- Not coming to a dead stop at a stop sign (stop means stop!)

Not moving off under control

- Rolling back on an uphill start
- Moving off with handbrake on
- Trying to move off in neutral
- Moving off in wrong gear
- Repeated stalling

Mistakes at junctions or when turning

- Improper mirror signal manoeuvre
- Unnecessarily cutting corners
- Mounting the kerb

Road positioning/normal driving

- Driving too far from / too close to kerb
- Not driving in a bus lane when allowed and safe to do so
- On a roundabout creeping forward beyond the white line, whilst waiting for an opportunity to enter. (deemed as being in a position likely to cause another vehicle to alter course. Serious Fault)
- Straying across lanes on a roundabout.
- Not increasing or decreasing speed according to road signs. (Deemed as lack of awareness)

Not maintaining control/steering

- Erratic /jerky
- Crossing hands

- Striking a kerb

- Not having both hands on the wheel where possible (two hands)

Not responding to signals

- Not moving off on a green filter arrow when safe to do so

- Not going on a green light when safe to do so

- Driving through a red light

- Not reducing speed on approach to traffic lights (failure to show caution)

Use of mirrors

- Not checking prior to signal, manoeuvring

- Not being fully aware of cyclists and overtaking motorcyclists

- Not checking mirrors often enough

- Not being seen to check!!! (move head)

Moving off /safety

- Not checking mirrors, blind spot and road ahead.

- Incorrect indicating

Reversing excercise

- On approach. Positioning the vehicle too far forward

- During. Hitting cones

- Finishing. Failing to position rear of vehicle inside the required zone (remember to fasten seatbelt)

Correcting Bad Habits

To pass the test you will have to drive in a certain way adhering to all the rules. Demonstrate a high ability to concentrate, attention to detail, a high level of control over the vehicle and good road sense and road manners.

Bad habits built up over time can easily be your undoing on the test day. They don't just disappear overnight. Either get rid of them or be aware of which ones prevail and could effectively be your Achilles heel on the day.

Usual culprits that scupper people are incorrect mirror signal manoeuvre:

Using crossed hands instead of shuffling the wheel,

Poor choice of gears,

Tailgating other vehicles,

Poor road positioning,

Erratic steering and braking,

Incorrect road speed,

Forgetting to signal on entering and exiting a roundabout,

Pulling out in front of other vehicles leaving them insufficient room,

Pulling away from the curb without checking the blindspot/looking over their shoulder,

Lack of anticipation,

Improper handbrake use,

Poor reversing skills

The Solution

Make a concerted effort to practice away the old habits. During the few weeks leading up to the test, drive your car or van as if it's examination day. Make driving to the rules become second nature. Not having to worry about making mistakes due to bad habits will free up more headspace and concentration for all of the other necessary details of the exercise. Note if you have a car- fold up the interior mirror and use side mirrors.

Driving Test Tips and Scenarios

Anticipation/Observation/Assumptions

Anticipate what will and might happen next and keep planning ahead. Traffic conditions are unpredictable .You never know what's going to happen next or what could be around the next corner, roundabout or at the next junction. During the test there will be certain situations that you can expect and shouldn't be surprised by. Examples are people walking into the road from a bus at a busy bus stop, or traffic light sequence at road junctions-if the light's been green for a while it's a safe bet that it's going to change. Another is pedestrians waiting at a crossing, if there's a crowd of people someone will have pressed the button, it's just a matter of time. Show caution on approaching zebra crossings. It's important to take extra care and be observant, particularly when the zebra crossing is close to an awkward junction or partially obscured by a large vehicle. Keep **scanning** the area for possible adults in a hurry on their phone, or young children stepping straight out oblivious in to the road.

Be **prepared** and fully aware of all other traffic. If you can't see round a corner then approach it slowly ready for the worst. At a junction where you can't see very well, emerge carefully, **observe** properly and don't assume the roads clear. Its better in fact to always expect the worst. Effective observations are very important in avoiding potential incidents and accidents. When meeting oncoming traffic on narrow roads, don't just think about the space you're going into but how you're going to get back out. Try constantly to think and be prepared for what's next. Consider what lorries may be hiding from your view and also traffic lights ahead and what's after the traffic lights. In a narrow road example situation, if you do not take it steadily, exercising caution and instead keep on heading into the middle of the road **expecting** the road to be clear you could run right into trouble and possibly have to reverse. Always plan ahead and expect the worst. Keep up your awareness and look out for any potentially unexpected situations. Remember, signs and road markings are all there to help you.

Concentrate and take in all the information around you including what you see in your mirrors and keep **planning** and **scanning**. Be aware of buses, cyclists passing on the (nearside) inside and motorcycles and emergency vehicles speeding by.

Look well ahead and try to spot road signs early so you have time to think and react. Be aware of dual carriageways ending and traffic merging or bus lanes, cycle lanes ending and traffic merging. All it takes is to miss the signs and road markings and you could end up driving the wrong way up a one way street or over the speed limit. If you're unsure what the speed limit is then look for the smaller repeater signs.

It is vital to anticipate and plan ahead .Also don't forget to keep checking the mirrors and being seen to check them and also checking the blind spot when pulling out or changing lanes.

In various situations such as these; try asking yourself; can I enter and exit the box junction before the lights change? Have any of the people at the pedestrian crossing pressed the button? Is it safe to go around the stopped bus or are there people starting to cross? Plan for what might and will happen next, it is very important to keep anticipating and planning. If you fail to keep doing this it is more than likely that mistakes will start to happen.

Assumptions. Don't assume the speed limits on the road your on are not going to alter, or that to go straight on at a roundabout you always have to use the left hand lane(mostly you do, sometimes you don't), or you can never drive in bus lanes or two in one lanes.

Never assume you have failed your test. When you make a mistake that totally puts you off, such as stalling when moving off. Don't continue on the test dwelling on what has just happened. If you do you will not be concentrating in the moment and may start to make more and more mistakes. Just let go of the past situation, recover from it and focus on what's next. Keep going. Be positive ...

Try not to be distracted by what the examiner is writing or if and when they speak . You don't know what it is they've written, and can't do anything about it anyway. Don't be distracted from the task in hand. Drive safely and within the law.

Note: Pre Test

Get to know the roads immediately in the vacinity of the test centre. This makes the start and end of test easier. Practice lots, learn from mistakes. Build up your experience. A pre-test mock test is recommended.

Take the test when you're ready and confident. Believe in yourself.

Nerves

Day of the Test

Most people get nervous. On the day of the test, try to keep to your normal routine. Eat breakfast. If you find your feeling butterflies in your stomach, still try to eat something. This will help to keep your energy levels up as nervousness tends to burn up a lot of energy. Ideally you don't want to be stressed by feeling hungry.

Prepare your day. No rushing around, have a calm day but stay occupied ...

It can be helpful to ease nerves by drawing confidence from experience. Remember all the preparation you've put in leading up to now.

All the effort, the hours spent behind the wheel and the on road experience you have.

Another good thing is to take a 45 minute pre test lesson. Talk to the instructor, re familiarise yourself with the vehicle, get into the driving zone.

If possible arrive at the test centre in plenty of time. If you still find yourself with an over active chattering mind, answer it with positivity using the knowledge you've gained up to now as an edge. "I'm used to focussing, I've put plenty of practise time in, I've got experience, I can do this etc".

Switch off your phone, then head into the test centre, ideally 5 to 10 minutes prior to test. Show proof of identity etc.

Walk out and ease yourself into the truck. Ease into the test.

Start steadily. Once you get going focus will concentrate the mind and help to ease nerves.

Note

In case your throat gets dry having a bottle of water with you is a good idea.

To Summarise

Stack the odds in your favour by:

choosing the best driving school

Assessing test centre entrance and exit

learning most of the route

driving the route

knowing the difficult junctions

knowing the speed limits

keeping the same vehicle

overcoming bad habits

anticipation, forward thinking of the road

anticipating other motorists intentions

avoid lack of road progress

avoid hesitancy, where appropriate keep the wheels rolling

stop at stop signs (stop means stop)

knowing the highway code

focus focus focus

confident calm and concentrated

Conclusion

I fully understand how time-consuming and expensive it is to gain an lgv licence. I also understand that everyone is different. What works for one person may not work for another. I recommend you cherry pick from the information provided, whatever works best for you. I hope this chapter helps with the challenge of passing your test.

Summary

I hope that you have found this book a useful guide to the world of trucking. Remember to revise the example examination questions if you decide to switch to a different company.

I want to leave you with a final piece of advice. Remember not to rush. It is easier said than done. You may be employed by people who try to pressure you into completing more deliveries than are legally possible in the time allocated. However, rushing leads to mistakes. Excessive risk-taking carries potentially dangerous consequences. Whether you have 1 delivery or 50, if they don't get done due to circumstances beyond your control, they don't get done. Your licence and personal safety are far more important.

On the road you will encounter many potentially stressful situations. You cannot control these situations, but you can control your reaction to them. If you stay calm and focussed, you are far more likely to come home safe and happy at the end of the day.

Acknowledgements

With very special thank-yous for all your help!

Danny Omz
Cody
Donna Hamilton
Michael Kingston
Uri Freixa
Nick Cosstick
Chris Bradley

Photo contributors:

Bob Spears
Marko Kudjerski
Triston
Arham Javed
Babish
Daniel Rosenberg
Hafez Thaikulathil

If you would like to contribute to the next edition and for general enquiries please contact jellymantrucking@yahoo.co.uk.

Thank you to ASDA avonmouth depot Bristol.

Recommendations

A very special thank you is reserved to a few trucking vloggers who've shown exceptional intent in helping new drivers . These vloggers understood the concept behind the book. By backing the project they've helped to raise awareness and I'm grateful to them. Their vloggs are interesting and a great source of information .
I can definitely recommend these vlogs.
Trucker Jay in the UK
Luke C in a HGV
KevTee-UK Trucking Diaries

Note to Reader

I am trying to raise awareness of this handbooks existence. If you have found this handbook useful and informative please let other drivers know of its existence either by review on Amazon, a mention on forums or word of mouth etc.

Gallery

Arham Javed

Babish VB

Bob Spear

Lightning Source UK Ltd.
Milton Keynes UK
UKHW022119091120
373107UK00002B/16